POETRY RE\

S U M M E R   2 0 0 1   V O L U M E   9 1

EDITOR PETER FORBES

PRODUCTION JANET PHILLIF

ADVERTISING LISA ROBERTᴐ

CONTENTS

Seven Years On: A New Generation Retrospective – Part 2

All illustrations by Gerald Mangan

THE SOCIETY OF AUTHORS

Eric Gregory Awards
2002

Annual awards totalling up to £24,000 for the encouragement of young poets.

A candidate must be British by birth, under the age of 30, and may submit a published or unpublished volume of poetry (up to 30 poems).

Closing date 31 October 2001

Full details and entry form from:
Awards Secretary
The Society of Authors
84 Drayton Gardens
London SW10 9SB
Please send SAE.

POETRY REVIEW
SUBSCRIPTIONS
Four issues including postage:

UK individuals £27
Overseas individuals £35
(all overseas delivery is by airmail)
USA individuals $56

Libraries, schools and institutions:
UK £35
Overseas £42
USA $66

Single issue £6.95 + 50p p&p (UK)

Sterling and US dollar payments only. Eurocheques, Visa and Mastercard payments are acceptable.

Bookshop distribution:
Signature
Telephone 0161 834 8767

Design by Philip Lewis
Cover by Janet Phillips
Cover image © PhotoDisc, Inc

Typeset by Poetry Review.

Printed by Newnorth Print Ltd at Newnorth House, College Street Kempston, Bedford MK42 8NA
Telephone: 01234 341111

POETRY REVIEW is the magazine of the Poetry Society. It is published quarterly and issued free to members of the Poetry Society. Poetry Review considers submissions from non-members and members alike. To ensure reply submissions must be accompanied by an SAE or adequate International Reply coupons: Poetry Review accepts no responsibility for contributions that are not reply paid.

Founded 24 February 1909
Charity Commissioners No: 303334
© 2001

Funded by
THE ARTS COUNCIL OF ENGLAND

EDITORIAL AND BUSINESS ADDRESS:
22 BETTERTON STREET, LONDON WC2H 9BX

telephone   020 7420 9880   fax 020 7240 4818
email   poetryreview@poetrysoc.com   ISBN 1 900 771 27 6
website   http://www.poetrysoc.com   ISSN 0032 2156

The Poetry Society is supported by

BT

MIMI KHALVATI

Mimi Khalvati is unusual in today's poetry climate in writing gentle, intensely aesthetic formal poetry. John Killick, in his essay on Khalvati in *Poetry Review*, Vol 85 no 2, 1995, compared her to Wallace Stevens for her interest in the musical metaphysics of verse. Some of the delicacy of her poetry undoubtedly derives from her Iranian background: the "Mirrorwork" of the book of that name (Carcanet, 1995) refers to the mosaics which decorate Iranian shops and palaces. Her latest book, *Entries on Light* (Carcanet, 1997), is a set of meditations on light. The poems relate both to Western painters, especially the Impressionists, and to eastern philosophy: "Who can tell on water / if shadow's nibbling into light / or light a shadow's edge?" Khalvati grew up on the Isle of Wight and it is this background that informs her forthcoming collection, *The Chine*, to be published by Carcanet in the autumn.

THE CHINE

To be back on the island is to be
cast adrift but always facing the same
mother who stays ashore, is always there
despite the mist. My balcony's a crib.
Through its bars the waves rush in. Not a ship,
not a gull, and the sky in its slow revolve
winding the Isle of Wight with a giant key.

We are spinning backwards in a slow spin;
we are in a time warp, a gap, a yawn,
a chine that cleaves the mind in two, a line
on the land's belly. Shanklin. Rhylstone Gardens
where an old man rolls tobacco, as spare
with the strands as the years have been with him.
Luccombe with its own chine, barely a stream.

Every childhood has its chine, upper world
and lower. Time itself seems vertical
and its name too implies both bank and stream.
To be back on the island is to walk
in both worlds at the same time, looking down
on talus, horsehair fern notched through the Ice Age,
Stone Age, Bronze Age and still here at our heels;

looking up like an elf, ears cocked to silence,
from a zigzag of silver and silt. A chine
is a form of urgency to reach the sea.
As coastlines have eroded, chines, like orphans
stranded in a high place without their slope
of history, have had to take a short cut,
make deep cuts into the soft clay of cliffs.

Childhood has its railings too. And its catches
of glove on rust, twisted wire with a slight give.
Playthings. For in an upper world that turns
beachfronts into toytowns, patches of moss
into stands of minuscule trees, no railing
is not a harp, no rung a wind might play on
something other than its maker intended.

Every leaf must be touched and tasted, holly
tested for suppleness, mimosa dusted.
The mind has its work cut out by the senses
and analogies must be drawn, the unknown
be known a friend by citing its kith and kin.
Shanklin. I know you as you were, the timbers
of your pier, now gone, of your tree-stormed bridges.

But in the lower world we dream. We listen.
Not for water which is the sound of listening
or for schoolgirls passing above unseen.
Under lawns, hotels, we sit hours midstream,
crouched under a hundred blankets. If eyes
were ears, we'd hear the very mud-bed thicken,
rise in little mounds where the water's clean.

Every path brings us back to the beginning.
Shanklin Chine is closed for the winter, both ends
barred with notices. But the mind is not.
Or memory. And time is spinning backwards
with the mainland out of sight and the great plain
where herds roamed the floor of the English Channel
and were drowned by it flush again with valleys.

I look down on them, my own that were fed
by chines, from the long esplanade of light
on Keats Green and seem to remember walking

with my mother here, running my hand on railings.
The beautiful inn on the corner's a wreck
and there, at the bend, where the light's so bright
and people walking down the steep incline

pause at the top before walking down, black
against the blaze before their torsos sink,
something vanishes, there, where the path drops
and a young boy comes running down the hill.
Never, O God, to be afraid of love
is inscribed on a new bench where I sit,
facing the headland with its crown in mist.

W N HERBERT

W N Herbert defies most normal categorizations. Fiachra Gibbons
made a game try when he called his poetry, "A weird mix of Desperate
Dan, McDiarmid and Dostoevsky". His most recent book *The
Laurelude* (Bloodaxe, 1998), written when he was writer in residence at
Dove Cottage, weaves fantastications around *The Prelude*, Laurel and
Hardy, William Burroughs and much else besides. Its predecessor,
Cabaret McGonagall (Bloodaxe, 1996), was, as the title suggests, a galli-
maufry of contemporary street language and synthetic Scots: "Fur aa
that's cheesy, static, stale, / this place gaes sae faur aff this scale / o ony
wigwam Bam-meter / mimesis wad brak thi pentameter". Synthetic
Scots is Herbert's most famous achievement, taking off from
MacDiarmid obviously, but in the end distinctly Herbertian.
Omnivorousness is his defining trait: everything, high or low, that he
encounters seems to be grist for his mill.

THE CHRONICLE OF RONNY GILL

Poor Ronny Gill is missing and
they'll never track him doon:
hear them shouting in the shadows
and the tunnels of the Toon –
there's a mannie stood at Monument
his job is just to croon
Ronny Gill

They've searched in aal the cellars and
they've looked in each saloon,
they dragged the Tyne to Blaydon
and they foond a silver spoon
that's never known the knackered mooth
of the man that has to croon
Ronny Gill

Some say he's gone to Metroville
some say he's on the moon,
some say he used to be a man
and now he's a baboon
but there's a gentleman at Monument
whose task is just to croon
Ronny Gill

Some say he's wor Pied Piper
some say he's Daniel Boone
and the Alamo won't let him go
until he names that tune
and there's a long lost soul at Monument
that's howling like a loon
Ronny Gill

When did he leave where did he go
and will he be back soon?
For coal and Keegan, ships like rats,
he's danced them from wor Toon
and left a man at Monument
with a single speech balloon
Ronny Gill

Note: The Chronicle *is the local Newcastle paper, sold with the aid of this approximate cry.*

CLARE POLLARD

Clare Pollard published her first poems in *Poetry Review*, was a featured poet in the magazine in 1996 at the age of 17, and published her first collection at 19: *The Heavy Petting Zoo* (Bloodaxe, 1998). Then she went to college – Cambridge University. Her subject matter is the typical concerns of an adolescent girl but her sensibility is unusual. Few adolescents have the verbal skill to describe what they're going through and Clare Pollard has a strong measure of self-reproach. The horrors of bad parties, even bad kissing, have never been so minutely dissected as they are in *The Heavy Petting Zoo*: "...filling your throat / with its unknown glue-juice / until you want to hide / slug pellets behind your lower teeth". Selima Hill has said of her work: "This is work you can't ignore – raw, reckless and more bloody-minded than an older, so-called wiser poet would dare to be". She has recently made a poetic documentary for Channel 4's Alt-TV – *The Sixteenth Summer* – and is currently writing a novel, *Love Spelt Backwards*.

HALLELUJAH

Sand stretched out like the margin of a parchment.
My mouth was a wineskin, drained.
Dust clutched at my soles, as I paused to cool

in the door-frame's shadow,
in silent adoration of Mary – her fumbling grace.
She was beside the window, kneading,

her palm-leaf eyes still onion-wet –
a hymn beneath her breath.
It's hard to explain how it all. . . It was so sudden –

how the sun struck her tan cheek; soft, dark hairs stuck
to its film of sweat. Stumbling,
she cuffed the clay jug of milk

and whitened the room,
and took in a gasp of joy, on her knees now.
I make things from wood. Carved tongue fits exactly

into groove. That face was incandescent, perfect
with a beauty that I could only gape at:
could not work up with my hands.

The air in the line of her eyes held specks of dust, skin, her;
they blended and danced like stars in the shaft of light,
above the table that I had made.

TOURISM

Spain was gold as saffron, and Borolo red,
a fat moon in the sky, and sangria-soaked head.
Sitting at wooden bars and ordering jamon,
blood-sausage, the terrible violence of the sun

as it mapped tender countries out onto my back,
and curtains drawn at noon in the room where we'd fuck.
Then the bullfight, the beast's wide neck wholly pierced through,
it spinning in madness' labyrinth as though

on heat, the strutting matador's cape draped before
its stagger, luring its fierce weight to the dust floor.
Quietened, I drank warm Cruz Campos, took photos,
soberly watched the corpse dragged off, and clapped, and rose.

But these memories only return to me as willed –
it is your face, your touch, that floods back though uncalled:
you splayed out, feverish and sleepy in the shade,
or racing over burning sand; how you tasted

when our daily picnic of bread and chorizo
spiced up your tongue, or how when on the pedalo
I threw up, you took my abuse all the way back.
The suntan and sucking mosquitoes left no mark,

but you did, you do, and the only trips I take
which matter are to get to you – those weekend breaks
next to your heart, and though I never will possess
the real you, and we will remain as foreigners

my use of love never translating into yours,
I can make do with the snap-shots that I have stored:
thumb through them at night, in the darkness, when a sea
of silence rushes in to estrange you from me.

PHILIP GROSS

Philip Gross has a quicksilver animistic descriptive gift which has some-times confused readers. He was initially mistaken – even by Craig Raine – for a Martian and certainly he could pull off the Martian trick when he wanted to. Three collections under Faber's Martian imprint followed and when it was finally realised that he wasn't a Martian at all, he left for Bloodaxe. The plasticity of his imagination and his chameleon nature have prevented critics getting a proper handle on what he is doing. His latest collection, *The Wasting Game* (Bloodaxe, 1998) has poems about his daughter's anorexia and his exploration of Estonia, his father's birth-place. Sorting out what survives of the earlier phase and what kind of poet he really is will be helped by the forthcoming selected poems, *Changes of Address* (Bloodaxe, September).

LOSING IT

What was it, that if *one* can,
in the old Guinness ad, *think what toucan*
do? And what is it that, gone,
a word leaves? Something like a token
of obscure esteem, or love, or
sense, like the dusting of stale talc in
an empty dresser drawer –
ungraspable, and yours for the taking

into that forgetfulness we all
might come to. Then we'll see what two can
truly do. I think the word
was *satisfy*, but I could be mistaken.
Shut me up, love. Hold me.
Sometimes I can't hear myself for talking.

NOCTURNE

Of all the times in all the nights in all the world
to have a blackbird singing . . . Of all the monochrome

stills of small hours smuggled as the clocks go forward
stealing a march on us, into the notion of spring . . .

Of all the side-slips into half waking, into half now
like a module, one bed's width, with its own supplies of air

and wonder — or like a lifeboat adrift for weeks
where we've rigged up a tenting of polythene sheet

creased so our breaths condense and trickle back down
to a taste flat as battery water, just a hint of tar,

salt and Swarfega . . . Of all these night-moves,
these casual pick-ups of logic, quite fuzzy and plausible,

that lead down a back street of connections
where the one lamp fizzes orange, melting wall,

roof, binbag, me, you and a low cat into its dream
and one blackbird can't sleep, and we should really do

something about the thin curtains that let in a glimmer
to touch in your cheek, eyes closed, eyelids quivering,

lips in the consideration of a smile . . . Of all the faces,
I had to wake into yours, at last, here's looking at you,

looking all the ages that you've ever been
and that blackbird, time switch blown by the always

not quite dawn, in the scrub of the railway cutting
sings as if there's no tomorrow, or no night between.

BRIAN HENRY

Brian Henry is one of the new breed of international poet-editor-critics. He teaches at the University of Georgia, is an editor of *Verse* magazine (once UK, now US), has published a first collection in the UK (*Astronaut:* Arc, 2000) and has worked in Australia. Roddy Lumsden has identified Henry's characteristic trait: he doesn't have one. Unlike British poets for whom "the voice" is the thing, Henry changes register often. So, superficially, his work can resemble post-Ashberian games but his solid grounding in the mainstream poetry world gives his poems an edge of plangency and soul that experimental work often lacks. In its playing with syntax that sounds as if it means something even if the meaning is elusive, *Astronaut* is reminiscent of the early work of Glyn Maxwell: "Never mind the fantasy about the tweezers and the tongue, / the one about the bicycle pump and the twisted rim. / Never mind the angle of penetration, or the number / of blessed repetitions in the series of withdrawals and goings-in".

VOICES LIKE THIS

I resist this beginning and hope it does not last.
I resist it because I have no place at the start.

My preference is to wash the landscape down with a stare
before stepping into what I have established.

Hence my love for rivers, for any water that's moving.
Hence my resistance to the I's presence too soon.

If I could wear what I hear the world would own me.
As I own nothing I try to hear what is said to me.

One could say I move in a different country.
One could say I have lost the urge to listen.

This would explain some of what requires explanation.
One could call this a virtue. One could call it a sin.

The words on the phone, because I could not catch them,
severed me from those who spoke them.

The woman in front of me, her knee
has withdrawn beneath the table as if to conceal.

If I were crouched beneath the table
the words I'd hear would match the words I would say.

The music of her legs, an exhalation I'd embrace,
would produce a note that, when repeated, I'd understand.

I support understanding. I support communication
between the mouth and the leg, the mouth and the mouth.

It should not surprise that I support communication
between the mouth and the cunt, the mouth and the cock.

If a mouth seeks congress with an ass, an ass with a cock,
I support the understanding sought. And so

with the meeting of mouth and breast, breast and cock.
The table's role in this is clearer than when I began.

If I were seated there she would know I have no secrets.
The secrets I have interest only me.

If she asked me to tell her something interesting
I'd feel the pull of narrative, the nostalgia it brings.

I would be forced to admit I know nothing of interest.
I prefer this to inventing a tale for the purpose.

Her knee has not emerged from the table
where, I've noticed, she sits alone.

Of course she is enveloped in blue, her hair brown as it descends.
It descends past her shoulders, the collarbone I can see.

Because I have no language I must repeat what I hear.
She says nothing, I have no words to repeat.

If she moves her knee into view I will approach.
If she moves her mouth as if to speak I will repeat the motion.

The silence the phone has brought between us
has not brought us closer.

It is no strange thing to have the look of prayer
when a body is the main concern.

Because her body is the main concern
there can be no part of her I will not revere.

My mouth when it moves will move for her.
This posture I offer to bring me closer.

I am no closer than when I began.
Because her tongue, like her knee, remains unseen

I maintain the posture. I must step to her and motion
as if my mouth to move. I must step to her

and motion as if my mouth to move.

CIARAN CARSON

Ciaran Carson has managed an unusual marriage in his work between the Irish vernacular story-telling tradition and the witty, elusive mock-pedantic scholarship of Paul Muldoon. Like Muldoon's, Carson's work is intensely allusive. In much of his poetry he has a project of sociological scope: to evoke Belfast in encyclopaedic detail. In *Belfast Confetti* (Bloodaxe, 1990), the Belfast of the Troubles is mapped with obsessive precision and the language of urban disturbances is as powerful a presence as the Troubles themselves. In his next book, *First Language* (Gallery, 1993), which won the T. S. Eliot Prize, language has become the subject. There are translations of Ovid, Rimbaud and Baudelaire. Carson is deeply influenced by Louis MacNeice and he includes a poem called 'Bagpipe Music'. What it owes to the original is its rhythmic verve. Carson then entered a prolific phase in which the concern for language liberated him into a new creativity. Translation became a key concern: *The Alexandrine Plan* (Gallery, 1998) featured sonnets by Baudelaire, Rimbaud and Mallarmé rendered into alexandrines. His translation of Dante's *Inferno* will be published by Granta next year.

DANTE: INFERNO

CANTO V

So I descended from the First into
        the tighter Second Circle: here, less space
        but greater pain, so louder screams ensue.

Minos the terrible, with grinning face,
        squats on the threshold; here he tries the crime,
        and girds himself according to each case.

For when it is another wretch's time
        to come before him, he confesses all,
        and then this judge performs a clever mime:

allocating him a place in hell,
>he coils his tail as many times around
>himself as grades that soul is doomed to fall.

Continually they come within his bound;
>each criminal in rota is arraigned;
>they tell; and then they're somersaulted down.

"O you who come to the abode of pain!"
>cried Minos, as he fixed his eye on me,
>abandoning the rule of his domain,

"mind how you enter, mind with whom you be,
>let not the wideness of the gate deceive!"
>Then said my guide, "What means this ignorant plea?

Do not impede him who is fated to achieve;
>for what is willed is what is in our grasp
>to will to be; so now we'll take our leave."

With that, the doleful notes begin to rasp
>my consciousness; I've come into a zone
>where pain's expressed by shriek and moan and gasp,

where not the feeblest ray of light is known,
>which squalls and bellows like an ocean tempest
>when the waves are driven by the cyclone;

this infernal, never-ending blast
>drives every soul before it in its sweep,
>tormenting them with every turn and twist,

who, when they come before the ruin, weep,
>and gnash their teeth, and moan, and curse and swear,
>and blaspheme God, and bawl, and howl, and shriek.

And then I knew such torments are incurred
>by those who like to practise carnal sin,
>when reason is by furtive lust ensnared.

As starlings, when the evenings draw in,
>assemble in tremendous seething flocks,
>so are those dark souls gathered by the wind,

and hurtled to and fro in random flecks,
  devoid of hope of rest, or rest from pain,
  to which they are eternally transfixed.

And as the cranes go honking by in trails
  across the sky, so did those shadows travel,
  uttering the loneliest of wails;

whereat I said, "Who are these wretched people,
  Master, whom the black air flails and lashes,
  till their very being seems unravelled?"

"The first of these, who were enslaved by passion",
  he replied, "was empress of a thousand
  tongues, for she was Queen of Babylon;

So gross was she, to lechery so hardened,
  that she made her lust into a law,
  and hence absolved herself of what is banned.

Her name is Semeramis, bawdy widow
  of King Ninus, as the books relate;
  she ruled the lands ruled by the Sultan now.

Then comes one whose passion was so great
  she slew herself, that's Dido; Cleopatra's
  next, who had a corresponding fate.

See Helena, for whose sake the wars
  rolled on for years; and see Achilles bold,
  who fought with love, and lost out to its laws;

see Paris, Tristan" ; and a thousand other souls
  he showed me, pointing, giving out the names
  of those who died for love in days of old.

When he had finished allocating blame
  to all those ancient dames and cavaliers,
  a rush of pity caused me to exclaim:

"I fain would to that twosome speak, who steer
  so lightly by the starless wind, they seem
  a drifting gondola and gondolier!"

He answered: "Wait until the swirling stream
        has brought them closer; then entreat them by
        that love which leads them, and they'll not retreat".

Then, as the current whirled the spirits high
        above our heads, I raised my voice and cried,
        "O come and speak to us, if none deny!"

As doves, with wings extended, paraglide
        the air; when, summoned by desire, they swoop
        into their nest like loving groom and bride;

so did these spirits veer from Dido's troop,
        and flutter towards us through the dark decline,
        answering my pity with their truth.

"O living creature, gracious and benign!
        who travels through the void to visit us
        whose bloody limbs on earth were intertwined;

were He our friend who rules the universe,
        we'd pray to Him to grant you all His peace,
        since you have pity on our fate perverse.

Now you may hear and speak of what you please,
        and we will hear and speak with you a while
        since now the howling of the wind has ceased.

The town where I was born is maritime;
        here the mighty Po, his journey run,
        with his attendant streams is reconciled.

Love, which is so catching, seized this one
        for that fair body which they robbed me of;
        it still disturbs me, how the deed was done.

Love begets love; I was seized by love
        for him in turn, which gave me such delight,
        that as you see, we still are hand in glove.

Love brought us one death. He who took our life
        will burn in the abode of Cain".
        These were the words they said, which now I write.

And when I heard those wounded souls complain,
　　I bowed my face, and held it low until
　　the Poet spoke, and asked me, "What pertains?"

And I replied, "Alas! what kind of thrill,
　　what longing led them to that sorry pass?
　　And when did they their vital souls imperil?"

So I turned again to them, and asked:
　　"Francesca, all your torments make me weep
　　with grief and pity, whether now, or past;

but tell me, did you wake, or did you sleep,
　　and did you sigh, when Love breathed in your ear
　　of secret joys, so dubious and deep?"

And she: "There is no greater pain, I fear,
　　than to recall past joy in present hell;
　　and this is known by your overseer.

But since you want so desperately to dwell
　　on how and when our passion was begot,
　　then I'll be one of those who weep and tell.

One day, to pass the time, we read of Lancelot,
　　who loved illicitly. Just the two of us;
　　we had no thought of what, as yet, was not.

From time to time that reading urged our eyes
　　to meet, and made our faces flush and pale,
　　but one short moment overcame our lives.

For when we read of how the longed-for smile
　　was kissed by such a noble knight, the one
　　who for eternity is by my side

all trembling kissed my trembling mouth. The man
　　who wrote the book was Galeott. O such a book!
　　That day the rest of it remained unscanned".

And while one half of this fond pair so spoke,
　　the other wept so much, I fainted. All
　　of me was overwhelmed by that stroke

of pity; and I fell heavily, as a dead man falls.

SELIMA HILL

Selima Hill is absolutely *sui generis*. She approaches everything from a different angle to anyone else. This note is hard to characterize but rueful/assertive/mischievous complaints against the world, and especially men, wouldn't be too far off the mark: "When you had quite finished / dragging me across your bed / like a band of swaggering late-night removal men / dragging a piano / the size and shape of the United States of America..." Fiachra Gibbons has said of her: "She has an edge, and always seems capable of bundling you into the Ladies and doing something unspeakable with a billhook". In her hands, human behaviour has always attracted some odd similes but in her new poems the comparisons stretch even further. Her forthcoming collection, *Bunny* (Bloodaxe) is the PBS Choice for Autumn.

PORTRAIT OF MY EX-HUSBAND AS A CHICKEN-RUN

Chicken-runs are my idea of heaven.
Nobody minds if the place is falling apart;
and the pea-brained chickens wander up and down
leaving their eggs in all the wrong places
and trampling on their dinner
but who cares?
Every time they stab a little bug
they know the world was made for their delight;
for what could be more charming and convenient
than slipping behind a trail of Morning Glory
to bathe in dust as warm and soft as turtle-doves
before retiring to a quiet nest?
If only You had had the sense, O Lord,
to turn my husband into a chicken-run,
this whole distressing affair
would never have happened.

PORTRAIT OF MY EX-HUSBAND AS A DISTANT MOUNTAIN

If I think of my mind
as a sort of landscape, or moonscape,
there's always this stupid mountain in the way,
like one of those self-important distant mountains
seen from the cool verandahs of small hotels
that you wake up one day and decide you have got to climb,
but not being one of those enterprising types
loaded with priceless cameras and ingenious picks
who like nothing better than solid rock to grapple with,
I did not like it when I got up close –
and wished I'd gone for a much less mountainous mountain
where tiny birds and goats,
alert and weightless,
follow paths that are three-quarters air.

EVA SALZMAN

Eva Salzman grew up in New York City and moved to southern England in her mid-twenties in 1985. She graduated from the Creative Writing Program at Columbia University, New York, and in many ways remains an American poet. She was a featured poet in *Poetry Review* in 1987 and her first collection, *The English Earthquake* appeared from Bloodaxe in 1992. Her work attracted attention quickly for its in-your-face boldness. Ian Gregson said, in the *LRB*: "Much of the pleasure comes from the way the poems build a picture of a coherent but entertainingly changeable personality – scathing, imaginative, dismissive, moved and baffled by desire". *Bargain with the Watchman* followed from Oxford Poets in 1997. She is now broadening her range. Her opera, *One Two,* developed by English National Opera Studio, was showcased at Greenwich Theatre in May. For the last two years, she has been a visiting writer at Wesleyan Writers Conference in the States. Currently a Royal Literary Fund Fellow at Ruskin College, Oxford, she is working on a novel, lyrics and a poetry collection which will appear in the States.

THE MUSE OF BLUES

I was using a carving knife
down any number of men.
Maybe it was someone I knew
way, way back when.

I was feelin' kinda blue.

I was in a considerable rush,
sweeping whole armies away
with a Straight and Royal Flush . . .
I was ace with rocks and lead,
cutting the giants to shreds
Give me a break, okay?

I was feelin' kinda blue.
Wouldn't you?

All that's for becoming the boss.
All that, to be having a ball
wondering what was it for.
To be laid on my nice pine floor,
flattened to the shape of a cross
and crying for them all.

BROOKLYN BRIDGE

(designed by Roebling and finished by his daughter-in-law Emily)

This one's mine: not the nail-less Bridge of Sighs
and not the one they damned as Iron Brute,
not trembling on its net of "wheres" and "whys"
nor a stage, where enemies or film crews shoot

but a hunkering church, grown from Gothic grey,
its cables spun from spiders bred in books.
That dark harp was made for me to play.
However dark, I couldn't help but look

at ever darker slights, their height and girth
stringing me high above the traffic's hum.
I was harnessed by a yoke of fear, from birth,
less myself while adding to that sum –

the way the architect's now ailing daughter
laid her father's body, right across the water

JOHN KINSELLA

"Work, John Kinsella can do that for us", opines Sean O'Brien in *Strong Words*. Whatever can he mean? Certainly, Kinsella is the most vigorous poetry activist ever seen in the country: I don't suppose any one person knows the full scale of his projects. What is most interesting poetically is his ecumenism: he operates equally within the mainstream and the world of the Cambridge experimentalists and if anyone can bring these together it is he. Poetically, his work is still rooted in Australia: rooted is appropriate because his poetry investigates the ecology of Australia and creates an epic of the land poisoned by agribusiness: "top-dressed soil exudes decomposing nitrogen". Les Murray (who knows his rural Australia) has said of him: "Wheatfires, salt hollows, lightning as a type of razor wire – here's an anamnesis of rural Australia, but a poet unafraid to honour it with the full stretch of his language". But perhaps it won't be long before he turns his hand to English antipastoral: there's no shortage of subject matter.

THE CHAMBERS: PRISON CELLS BENEATH THE NINETEENTH-CENTURY COUNTRY MANSION, WESTERN AUSTRALIA

1.

In a darkness without chemi-luminescence
to challenge definition, no space
for comparison, tremors unsettled
the bricks, but not enough
to bring the walls down,
implode the chambers.

Beneath the house
with its antiques
and grand piano
ballroom opening out
like an invitation,
they enclosed.

Excavate, disinter, dig.
Exhume. Light fractures
and exchanges: heat, prayer.
So deep you wouldn't
have heard a sound uptop

when prisoners devolved
into apparently random gradations
of pitch. The throat
a battered flute.

Unfamiliar birds
made as game birds,
field-fattened,
shrill in the ovens:
the black warrior's skin
stretched against the wall.
Body-heat tarnishing
architecture, the space
beneath, within.

2.

As a child led through narrowing passages
to the chamber with manacles and an altar,
that first sound of harpsichord,
Goldberg variations. Down there,
a radio is static: nothing
comes in. Static is pater familias,
though the Church of England
sings here. A FLUX, luminary, organ glow, the form
                    of the body: the pain and grief
                    settled ritual prison life, a river beds
                    and flows nearby, the seepage
                    depths and whisperings
                    caught in bricks, sand, stone.

3.

Father gave his sons transistor radios
when they first hit the market:
they heard America,
and the cousins visited that house again.
You should go there. We should
do it together. You'd be scared.
Voiceover. Lies. Submission.

4.

The country kitchen opened out,
small abundant gods gesticulated
from hot places, from the cool
of the cupboards. Heavy stone
and high roofs kept the driving summers
out: a stranger performed tricks
with fruit over the wooden floorboards.
He sang ballads. He dressed up –
sharp shoes, red dress, rouge –
and recited "The Man from Snowy River".

5.

Water damage. Speak trenched spirit,
impudent light of depth, pressure, crush.
Uptop sheep nudging at the garden.
An imported palm sways in the sear wind.
Speech in the morning. Evening sense
loses fathoms. We asked you here
to state your case: location,
coordinates. Movements
of the peoples.

6.

Accused, fruit falls
from the place of the eyes.
Lightning lit hilltops
and fire raced down. Below ground it was cool,
though they sweated. The house went up quickly.
Labyrinths of title deeds and planning permissions,
inheritance, death tax, changes in governments:
a compact whirlwind cut the garden,
cutting dates out of papers.
In the static it seeped in,
we know that all this is proof.
Proof: this theory, this transubstantiation:
the bells as confident as stone,
proof heard, turned to story.

Manufactured Environments

by Matt Barnard

JOHN KINSELLA

The Hierarchy of Sheep

Bloodaxe, £7.95
ISBN 1852245522

AS I'M WRITING this the first cases of foot and mouth disease have just been found in Scotland and Northern Ireland. Coming on the back of the BSE catastrophe, the foot and mouth outbreak is making a whole mass of people for the first time seriously question society's relationship with its environment. It is this relationship which is at the heart of Australian-born John Kinsella's *The Hierarchy of Sheep*, a fact signalled from the start by the collection's title in which the polysyllabic word "hierarchy", which has strong cultural overtones, is applied to an animal normally seen to embody a lack of formal structure. However, Kinsella is certainly not aiming his examination of rural life at a popular or mass audience. He uses words from a wide variety of contexts, from colloquial Australian to Latin, French, farming and science, many of which send the reader to a dictionary, and reflect Kinsella's interest in colonialism and diversity, two sides of a coin. Additionally, many of the poems are difficult to read and interpret, including the opening poem in the collection, 'Adaptation'. Written in short lines of free verse, the poem begins with an unidentified "chemical body / shielded by foliage", which interferes with "vampire finches" in the Galapagos, the islands that played such an important part in Darwin's researches. By the end of the poem we've been taken to English greenhouses where evolution is having trouble because of man's ability to maintain an optimum environment.

Reading these kinds of poems is a claustrophobic experience that feels a bit like trying to navigate a maze where the green walls are closing in around you. And like a maze, some of the poems seem artificially manufactured, not all of the images and metaphors hitting quite the right note. In 'Adaptation', species like the finches are described as "loving / others' histories / vicariously". I think I get the sense of this phrase, which is something along the lines of change being driven by the desire to imitate a more successful neighbour, but "vicarious" seems the wrong word because one does something vicariously, one doesn't love something vicariously. Other poems, such as 'Yew Berry' and 'Reversal', are more successful.

However, among the turgid, avant-garde poems are more traditional and lyrical ones, such as the finely-balanced 'Ice', which has the lines: "Further down the path shattered / sheets of ice disperse reflection: / your face, a branch, the stark / blue winter sky. A landscape / saturated with trigonometries". The poem contains words from a variety of contexts, but here there is space to breath and the images work. The clear rapid syllables of "trigonometries" naturally reflect the idea of the clean sides and angles that ice makes when it is broken. But by no means are the more accessible poems always more successful. The collection contains a play-poem called 'The Shooting Party' written in heroic couplets, which deals with the tensions within a group of farm workers, some of which are university students doing holiday jobs. The trouble is that although it starts in orthodox iambic pentameter, the verse quickly degenerates, sacrificing metre and colloquial language for the sake of rhyme. A character uses the phrase "is it within the law?", to ask if a kangaroo hunt is legal, because "law" rhymes with "before" in the previous line. This technical waywardness reinforces the impression that the characterisation is also weak.

The collection is dedicated to former Australian Prime Minister Paul Keating for the "Redfern Speech", which he made to launch Australia's celebration of the 1993 International Year of the World's Indigenous People. In it, Keating acknowledged the injustices suffered by the native Australian population at the hands of the incoming European settlers, and calls on the country to embrace the cultural diversity of its inheritance and learn from the Aboriginal people's attitude to life, art and not least their relationship with the land. In England, we get a very skewed image of Australia and Kinsella's challenge, which is to show the vast complexity of the country, is a difficult one. Reading *The Hierarchy of Sheep* gives a very different impression of Australia from the one Britain normally sees and measured against that criteria, despite its flaws, it is a successful collection.

PETER PORTER

One of the few decent things OUP has done for poetry in recent years was to give Peter Porter a fine 70th birthday bash for his two-volume *Collected Poems* in 1999. Not a crowd-pleasing poet, although his earlier satirical poems had a wide appeal, Porter's work has been quietly influential, especially on the Sean O'Brien school (see Porter's review of O'Brien in the last issue). George Szirtes has tried to encapsulate Porterland, which contains: "...all the apparatus of high culture...cats, Popes, domestic sorrow, Auden, money, conspiracies, torture chambers, concentration camps, consumer goods, sex, domesticity, agents of political oppression, seediness, dreams of welfare state Britain, corrupt institutions, great tracts of Shakespeare, the Bible and big encyclopaedias, the chatter of history as well as the chatter of the chattering classes". He remains as productive as ever. A collection of his prose, *Saving from the Wreck*, has just appeared from Shoestring Press.

THE UNDARKEN'D RAY

Even those wily moralists who guess
   The leaden casket is the one to choose
Attest that fate commands the boundaries
   Of marvels, tropes and ordinariness,
A rather squally way of documenting
   The past's not just another country but
Home to a species utterly remote.

As much as in Sci-Fi we live our lives
   In capsules pelting to the end of time,
Computers stalked by mutant bugs *en suite*,
   The voyage outward like the one within,
A wrapless darkness, and bold history
   An information screen where love and hope
Flare and switch off, ungravitational.

(Ask what they wore when, in Byzantium,
   Heraclius's men stepped from their ships;
Convene a council where the cheese is forced
   To testify against the worms; demand
Which Frock Coats spoke for Darwin and which wrote
   Him calumnies. You gaze into a panel
Neither comprehensible nor persuadable.)

Outside the wonders of a magic town,
    A prairie tabernacle of a Pale
Of Pico's Greek Debaters, mind addresses
    Its diurnal dismalness or at best
Some sexual chance, a kind examination,
    Or even Sunday when the sun turns on
Its taps and Ego-Lion lies down with Lamb.

Such are the brief pre-echoes of the Great
    And promised Revelation, the reason why
The questions must be asked. Observe the hoard
    Of artist-understanders filling books
And walls with inklings, are they in the right?
    Was Coleridge foxed by Knowledge's advance
Till what time death shall pour the undarken'd ray?

KIT WRIGHT

Kit Wright is one of the light verse masters, using a bravura verse technique to convey an impressive range of emotions: from knockabout farce to the deadly serious polemic of 'I Found South African Breweries Most Hospitable'. Most of his work was out of print for some time following the demise of Hutchinson's poetry list and his reputation has suffered from indifferent publishing. His selected poems, *Hoping it Might be So: Poems 1974-2000,* was published by the new publisher Leviathan this year. His plangent, lugubrious humour is instantly recognisable and, for all the contemporary smartness of his work, his sensibility often seems to belong to a more dignified and kinder age. The title poem of the new book bears this out, a heartbreaking plea for a place in which evil is somehow cancelled out and destroyed lives made whole again: "where the drowned men rise, walk back from the boats in the evening. / And the lost child sings on her new-made father's knee".

TRAMLINES

The city has a rhythm you seem to know.

A one-in-ten you laboured up,
As you come back down, appears to possess
Some braked momentum of its own,
Some ratcheted decelerant
And stay of foot and eye.

For the hills of Lisbon constitute a house
Where you move without anguish
Between the rooms of distinct floors.

Or you might prefer the Lift:
A travelling oak saloon inside a meccano
Cathedral tower will shoehorn you high above
The terracotta cataracts
And the pastel cliffs,

With here a Cézanne and there
An aeronautical Lowry.

Best of all might be one of the oval
Dolls' house trams with their brainy wands
To magic them, with a difficult magic,
Over and round and through the switchback course.

It is like a sometimes recalcitrant
Children's electric train set,
Needing a jog from time to time.

And the driver, working his live-man's handle
360 degrees through twelve positions,

Is never without a civilian
Consultant at his elbow,

To chew the fat and roust out cars in the way.

Or there's the other
Big Bendy Wender of a tram
With its double-concertina'd articulation,
Sashaying into a turn with rolling hips.

In any case,
You will want to be still
Under the olive trees on the battlements
Of the Castle of St George
With the mare's tail grass and poppies and hawkweed and mallow . . .

And gaze out at the blazing wide blue Tejo,
The sea of straw; likewise
Foundation-stone of the uncovered planet

For Here Comes Everything,
With its lateen sail and its astrolabe,
Its octant, or its Manueline
Artillary sphere,

Gunning for the mouth
Of what might be known.

Here comes Africa,
Here comes India,
Here come the Americas.

They were not, of course, lost,
That they needed to be discovered,

But here comes Most Of It,
And of course, one way and another,
Here comes Macdonalds.

VICKI FEAVER

David Thompson

Vicki Feaver's poetry has been characterized by Matthew Sweeney as "domestic gothic, where the women are sensual and murderous". There are just two books over a career of twenty years – *Close Relatives* (Secker, 1981) and *The Handless Maiden* (Cape, 1994) – but the poems make up in force for their lack of numbers. Several of the poems in *The Handless Maiden* are indeed preoccupied with the idea of murder: Judith begins "Wondering how a good women can murder..." and ends "And I bring my blade / down on his neck – and it's easy / like slicing through fish. / And I bring it down again, / cleaving the bone", and 'Lily Pond' begins "Thinking of new ways to kill you / and bring you back from the dead". If not all as stark as these, her poems tends towards raw rather than politely cooked emotion.

THE TRUNK

Later, when I heard the story
of all the evils of the world
unloosed from a box,

I thought of Grandma's trunk:
the shawl crocheted from wool
the colours of flames – orange

and mauve and gold – that lay
like a sleeping beast on top;
the bands of black metal

that held everything in;
and of her opening the lid,
pulling out the fox tippet

with dangling claws,
the bead-fringed brocade coat,
the bone teething ring

roughened with bite marks;
then letters and photographs –
Grandpa who'd died of pneumonia

caught at a football match, Jack
in a striped Rugby shirt, holding
a silver cup – everything she'd kept

to remind her of what was lost.
She was kneeling on the floor, sniffing,
wiping her eyes on her sleeve,

until there was nothing left
except the long white nightdress
she wanted to be laid out in,

and then mothballs, rolling
like peppermints along
the empty bottom.

THE MAN WHO ATE STONES

He had never felt so light:
his skin like the paper of kites,

bones like the inside of Maltesers.
He thought he was going to float

through the roof of the house,
drifting through space

like an astronaut
untethered from his craft.

He begged his wife to hold him down
but she just laughed.

He drove to the beach, and knelt
at the edge of the sea,

swallowing pebbles to weight
his stomach with ballast.

The water was black, except where the moon
lit fires in the breaking waves.

He saw the great grey molluscs,
feet clamped to the rocks,

grazing on streamers
of crimson weed;

and the god whose home
is under the ocean's storms,

the bubbles of his breath
shooting to the surface.

Here was another man
who had to eat stones.

Splashing into the burning water,
he waded to meet him.

ELIZABETH GARRETT

Alison Richards

Elizabeth Garrett was notable amongst the mostly street-wise New Generation for her adherence to a pure classical lyric line. Her work owes more perhaps to John Donne than it does to Douglas Dunn or any one writing since him. Having said that, the directness of her address, the buttonholing style, seen here in 'Orientations' is very modern. The diction is a million miles from Carol Ann Duffy but you can tell they're living on the planet at the same time. Her one book at the time of New Generation, *The Rule of Three* (Bloodaxe, 1991), was followed by *A Two-Part Invention* (Bloodaxe) in 1998. Her poetry is intense and allusive, sometimes riddling; it is also passionate. David Constantine said of *A Two-Part Invention*: "[Her poems] confront the man-in-the-street with the ungainsayable proof that the world is livelier, more beautiful, more hurtful, more demanding than he in his day-to-day-sloth and cowardice is willing to admit".

ORIENTATIONS

Drop heart
Drop I
Suspend the soul.
Banish hope, doubt and dark.

In place of loss
Plant seed.
Let a secret breathe
But never burn the page.
Respect rage.

Love birds
And anything that flies.
Inspect all leaves,
Their underside, their shade & blade & stalk.
Ignore small talk
Except of children, streams, or elves.

Love food
And anything that feeds,
The baby and the breast – the give & take, the taking
In the gift.
Honour the pip's bright packaging
The slow wise root

That mutters in the blood
For it is good.

And when the light unsheaths
A blade of grass,
Ten million lives away
A child breathes.
And in that breath
Drawn clean from the body's sheath
To trouble the wind's white music
This compass needle
Flickers on the quick.

THE JAVANESE BIRDCAGE

Isn't dreaming of a bird. It is
Suspended halfway to nowhere
By the pressure of its own airiness,
The swift pale parabolas
Of reed vaulting inwards
To the vanishing point of their source.
Through it the light pours
Catching the day's breath
In the tiny motes that flash
Like mica fish through its bars.

Reverse icon! A vessel of air,
It makes of a space less
Palpable even than absence
A shrine for the pilgrim heart
To worship in, setting the caged
Song free: and what *is* beauty
But supreme sufficiency of form?
Such craft as endlessly invites
Significance, holding to none,
Nor yet leaving the bird unsung.

LAWRENCE SAIL

Terry Matthews

Lawrence Sail is a poet of disturbed calm, the precise, lucid surfaces of his poems riding over a more turbulent swell of anxiety. The aquatic metaphor here is not accidental because the sea is one of Sail's emblematic subjects (his selected poems is called *Out of Land* – Bloodaxe, 1992). Sail is an intensely sacramental poet: in his hands snooker becomes divine cosmology and allotments "the last real estate of common prayer". Even arriving at an airport is seen as: "Litanies of departure? – Check-in, the catechism / of Security questions, the electric angelus / Of chimes, passport control, the gate..." His most recent collection, *Building into Air* (Bloodaxe, 1995), elaborates on Audenesque notions of the concept of the city. The extraordinary organic persistence of the city, even such an extreme case as Hiroshima, is celebrated: "Yet even here, / ...the city has fruited / into strange newness". A new collection, *The World Returning*, is forthcoming from Bloodaxe.

BLACK IN THE EARLY 1950S

For a start, the bags under Edgar Lustgarten's eyes
as he shook his jowls morosely towards the stalls
from his leather chair, a coal fire licking behind him –
Of all the cases that baffled Scotland Yard
surely none was more strange than that of the headless
body at Midhurst Station, one bleak winter night . . .

And then the film itself, in which an ambulance,
black, topheavy, with great silver hinges,
would career down the curvy drive of a private clinic
in which some unspeakable procedure would be performed
without anaesthetic. Only the imagination,
wincing, could get past the doors with their blind portholes.

In real life, it could be just as bad – a man
wrapped in red blankets and held in place with straps,
carried from a house in the street. Not a good colour.
The ambulance gleaming like a hearse, the silver trolley
shiny as a fish. We children gawped. They slid him
in on runners and shut him into the dark.

Back at the clinic, at the very moment when
the eyes above the mask narrowed, pitiless, and the hand
moved to make the incision, more sugar-crunching
of wheels on gravel – enter two black Wolselys
with alarms clanging, rocking on their springs as out
leapt squads of policemen, all in their smartest black.

In 1952, a month or so before Newcastle
won the Cup for the second year running, black went
ballistic. Even the wireless rigged up at school
had its square face wimpled in black cotton
for The Funeral. Voices were solemn, close to tears.
One boy fainted. The teachers wore black ties.

Looking back, though, it's clear that really nothing
we saw at the Gaumont, the Odeon or the Savoy,
or in the street, or heard on the wireless at school
could hope to outdo the black of the late forties –
the aftermath of war, the cat slinking
across the dazzling dark toecaps of Harry Lime's shoes.

KEN SMITH

Pete Stiff

Ken Smith has been a lone, distinctive voice on the scene for a long
time. He is something of an urban cowboy, often fetching up in border-
line places. The word rootless comes to mind: that is, he doesn't write as
Seamus Heaney does out of a settled background. Smith was ahead of
his time because this kind of urban rootlessness is becoming the norm.
He has created an imaginative ecotone between worlds, and an *alter ego*,
Eddie: "In my other life in another country / on the world's other side I
get by, just". He is drawn to the allure of temporary places, the road
between departure and destination: "This is another place I won't
remember /...I have been travelling fast / with that far shine on the road
ahead / and the wind over me". His latest collection, *Wild Root*
(Bloodaxe, 1998), is reviewed on p.35.

SOUTH

Picture a city in the mountains,
between one cordillera or another
squeezing the burnt air, like wet moss.

A city of flowers, blossom trees,
exotic fruit and so many beautiful women
the eyes glaze over, everywhere.

Every street a market, chant of
chiclet chiclet, mango mango,
in the street of the watchstrap sellers

a man selling powder singing *cucaracha*
cucaracha cucaracha through the traffic,
every lane a fast lane till it stops.

Zona vehiculo calmado: a joke,
as would be siesta in this city
where the traffic never sleeps.

Bus bus yellow cab bus yellow cab.
Horns brakes whistles backfires. And guns.
Thieves and so many one-legged beggars.

In the doorways of bars squinting
out into the sunlight gnarled old men
wearing machetes. Guns. Guns.

You could just die here in the crossfire.
Yo ya no soy yo. Dead for ever.
Ni mi casa es ya mi casa.

Out beyond the city the dead zone.
You are advised not to travel at night.
You can't get up to the mountains

amongst all that clean air,
but as the light falls sometimes the rain falls,
dry lightning on the high crests.

Suleyman in Europe

by Anna Wigley

KEN SMITH

Wild Root

Bloodaxe £7.95
ISBN 185224 461 5

JOURNEYS AND BORDERLANDS form the subject
matter of this collection: voyages east and west; the
shattered and reconstructed borders of central and
eastern Europe; and those journeys of the heart and
spirit that the poet makes in his many confronta-
tions with human suffering and loss.

Here the crossing of great distances somehow
closes them. For though they range across hundreds
of years and thousands of miles, these poems are
united by their encounters with life at the sharp
end: with people living on the edge, struggling to
endure, sitting out stripped existences in the
shadow of material and cultural poverty, uprooted-
ness and war.

The concern is always with paying attention to
the neglected, correcting cosy fantasies, and giving
a voice to the dispossessed. In 'Countryside Around
Dixton Manor, circa 1715', he repudiates the myth
of rural England as it is embodied in the painting of
the title. The wheatfields and Morris dancers belie
the truth: "all my lord's dream of himself / is a hired
man's painting: / same tale then as now / and this
he's not changed either: / the enrichment of the
rich – / impoverishment of the poor. / None but

the reaper will come to your door".

Such a resolute refusal of the prettifying image and comfortable lie is a constant throughout this collection. And yet the lyric impulse is there, clear as the blackbird's song that appears in several poems as a token of domestic peace. Ken Smith can't help writing poems that are beautiful, however savage and comfortless the subject. The mournfulness of a poem such as 'Narrow Road, Deep North', for instance, in which he takes a train back to the land of his youth, is inseparable from its starkly lovely images of "birds / in a glitter of flying and "the light off the cliffs / climbing out of the dull sea / into rainclouds". Likewise, in another sombre piece, 'Here', the poet confronts his own physical frailty in the image on a hospital monitor, and gives paradoxical delight by the aptness of his metaphors: "1 watch the grey map of my heart, the bent / ladder of the spine that outlasts it".

Wild Root gathers pace and strength as it goes on. The closing sections are powerful and impressive, showing the poet working at full stretch and yet with apparent effortlessness. The fluency and authority of Smith's voice increases, and his easy command of image and rhythm seem as natural as spontaneous speech. This lack of strain goes along with a sense of vital and urgent communication: here is a poet with more to say than most, and the capacity to say it.

The outstanding poem for me is the long piece, 'The Shadow of God', which depicts the progress of a sixteenth-century eastern warrior-ruler,

Suleyman, across the many lands he ravages and conquers. If Picasso had been a poet, this is how his 'Guernica' would have looked. Suleyman is a terrifying embodiment of megalomania and religious fundamentalism, convinced of his providential duty to lay waste all before him, leaving on the battlefield centuries after "a museum of bones in the thick boney / stew of each other". Juxtaposed with poems on modern war-torn Europe, 'The Shadow of God' seems to bridge the gap of four centuries: the fanaticism and barbarity, the pleasure in destruction, are unnervingly close to home.

The closing sections of the book focus on post-Communist Russia and the former Yugoslavia. Here are poems of desolation and ruin, of lost identities and vanished communities, of people existing in the rubble of their own lives. They make you feel that Ken Smith is at heart a European poet – in his seriousness of purpose and largeness of heart; in his tragic sense of history, but also in his darkly satirical humour. Near the end is a poem that playfully imagines the secret police as a "much misunderstood minority" needing our support and sympathy: "let us create a special homeland for them", suggests Smith, where "they could speak their own / incomprehensible tongues" and "cultivate their habits of watching / by watching each other". It is a poem that reproduces the resourceful irony we associate with dissident writers, making its point with wry understatement, its tone, both sorrowing and humorous, typifies the uncomfortable pleasures of this exceptional collection of poems.

DERYN REES-JONES

Deryn Rees-Jones's two collections, *The Memory Tray* (Seren, 1994) and *Signs Round a Dead Body* (Seren, 1998) established her as one the most interesting post-NewGen poets. In her early poems her mentor was obviously Carol Ann Duffy but her exuberantly romantic style seemed very much to capture the mood of a particularly female zest for life in the 1990s. Her poem, 'Making for Planet Alice', gave its title to Maura Dooley's anthology of new women poets in 1996, and established a mood: "Quietly, quietly / Take me to that strange place, by bus, by unicycle, / Helicopter, aeroplane. Let me sail to planet Alice in my heart, / My leaky coracle". She teaches creative writing and has written criticism, including a study of Carol Ann Duffy (British Council / Northcote House, 1999). She co-edited, with Alison Mark, *Contemporary Women's Poetry* (Macmillan, 2000). Her collection of essays, *Consorting with Angels: Modern Women Poets*, is due from Bloodaxe next year.

TRUFFLES

The Umbrian black truffle, a delicacy in these mulish towns,
was born, or so the Romans had it,
when lightning struck the earth, secreting a nugget

of heavenly fire in oak or hazel woods whose altitude and climate,
calcerous soils, combine to breed its heady strength,
its auras known by sweating housewives, perfumed chefs

to make electric any humdrum dish.
A fungus potent, so we read, as the pheromones
of two wild boars – known also for their sense of smell –

whose butchered testicles emit a scent more dangerous to some
than Japanese beetles, gypsy moths
or Circe with her plaited hair

who tosses acorns, feckless men, into the hot Aegean mud.
More pungent then, than mountain goats
whose cheese we daub on rounds of bread,

the amoretti which we dip in wine, or
hemmed with rosemary and mint,
the sunflower fields where,

like the truffle hunters, too, this burning
afternoon, we root out treasures for ourselves
until we've harvested each spore

from armpit, neck, from groin,
enthralled by subterranean gods
who now make dogs of us, or swine,

till we lie senseless in the dirt,
hearts splitting in the heat.

OWEN SHEERS

Owen Sheers had that rare thing in poetry: a dream debut. Andrew Motion's support (Sheers graduated from the UEA Writing Program) and Sheers' good looks ensured coverage beyond the usual outlets for a first collection from Seren. *The Blue Book* (Seren, 2000) received a fairly sceptical review in *Poetry Review* but his descriptive gift is undeniable. In 'Degas' we find "Head bowed, a woman plays the cello of her hair"; 'Lambing' produces this: "And then the slow hydraulic extraction, / Chinese eyes and the long ears pulled back / by the g force of the womb". 'Unfinished business' finds him mining an Armitage-like territory of dodgy characters; it concerns a guy who "...dropped a breeze block on some bloke's unconscious face, // attacked a teacher with a Stanley knife, threatened / to fill in his kids and fuck his wife". Sheers's is an impressive debut, the poetry confident, glittering and suggestive.

Y GAER
(The Hill-Fort)

Its only defences now, a ring of gorse,
sown with yellow in Summer,
its lights extinguished by Winter.

Beyond, the mossy gums
of trench and rampart,
gateways that open to the view only,

and a stone pile, marking the centre,
where my horse threatens beneath me,
jittery from the long gallop,

alert to this place, veins mapping under her skin,
over her twitching muscle;
her nostrils, full of smoking embers.

The land is three-sixty about you here,
inescapable, bald, an answer to any question.
A green cloth, stitched with river silver.

And so I understand why the man who lost his son
comes here only in bad weather.
When he can lean full tilt against the wind's shoulder,

take the rain's beating, the hail's pepper-shot,
and scream into the storm's body, into its wild heart,
finding at last, something huge enough to blame.

MAURICE RIORDAN

Nico Sweeney

Maurice Riordan at first seemed a quietly ruminative poet of the kind that Ireland produces effortlessly. His early work, published in *A Word from the Loki* (Faber, 1995) had great charm. 'The Table' constellates a marriage around the image of a table long sought but never attained: "...you can still see / somewhere inside it the original deal, / the plain altar still fit for household ceremonies". His best-known poem, 'Time Out', develops the nightmare fantasy of leaving his two young children in the house while he pops out to the corner shop; he imagines death and the slow unfolding horror as the children wake up. But it ends: "Let's get this dad in and out of the shop safely across the street, / Safely indoors again, less a couple of quid, plus the listings mags...". But besides this domestic note, he has also developed a powerful line of scientific enquiry, sometimes sounding like a modern Lucretius. He edited, with John Turney, *A Quark for Mister Mark: 101 Poems about Science* (Faber 2001), and his latest collection, *Floods* (Faber, 2000) reviewed on p.40, has several impressive scientific poems.

THE HOLY LAND

Father Burns gave us his greyhound pup, Basil,
to mind while he was away in the Holy Land.
Basil's track name was *Goldfinger*. When he ran
round the house, it was as if he appeared
at one gable before he was gone from the other.
We believed him the fastest hound in Christendom.

My mother was loth to vilify a beast
on whom the priest had pinned his hopes.
But when he rooted up the lilies we heard
That little bastard muttered under her breath.
And when we took him to Buttevant for trial
he froze at the sound of the electric hare.

Basil still streaked round the house – though Father Burns
was home, and had projected the holy sites
onto the schoolroom wall: Gethsemane, Calvary,
the Mount of Olives, basilicas and mosaics;
then the minibus north to Galilee – Cana,
Capernaum, the water on which He walked, Nazareth
where He grew up. There too was a basilica.

And the World Pauses

by Julia Copus

MAURICE RIORDAN

Floods

Faber £7.99
ISBN 0 571 20462 7

THESE ARE POEMS which delight in telling us things. Did you know, for instance, that "a single filament which is drawn unbroken / from the cocoon [of a silkworm] can measure a kilometre or more" or that "if you dig the ground after a downpour / you'll find it dry just under the sod"?

The book's epigraph – "Time is what keeps everything from happening at once" – sets the scene neatly for a collection of deft poems in which past and present co-exist and time is by turns condensed, disordered, interrupted and restored. In 'The Rug', a child is upset by an underlay of old newspapers which bear witness to the fact that he and his mother "overlap but we do not coincide, / all this before I was born . . ."; elsewhere another (ageing) mother "undoes the silver coil of her hair" so that "it falls loose like a wedding veil to her waist"; and in a field in Wales a man in the middle of lovemaking is momentarily puzzled as to whether it's "a split second or several months" since he last made love to this same woman in her flat hundreds of miles away.

Interestingly, Riordan cites Alice Munro – whose work is also known for its temporal shifts in narrative – as one of his main influences. The fact that Munro is a short-story writer rather than a poet should come as no great surprise: Riordan undoubtedly has a knack for storytelling. The opening poem, 'The Sloe', is a lengthy dramatic monologue occasioned by the discovery of the body of a stone-age man in Austria who died at the start of "a climatic glitch which lasted 5,000 years / until the thaw on the glacier two summers ago / brought him to our attention". A professor at the Institute to which the body is taken for analysis tells the tale of the man's struggle to survive following an injury

which "sent him above the tree-line, far from the settlements". The narrative, with its sparsely described mountain setting, creates a strong sense of isolation that invites the reader to empathise with the wounded man who "died really from being alone", and

> not from lack of discipline
> or the body's weakness, or not only,
> but because of the slight
> shortening of the odds which comes
> with the unexpected comfort of snow.

Further details revealing how hopelessly he fought for survival, "how in his plight / he couldn't string the green yew stave, couldn't ignite the tinder / to roast the songbirds", are intended to kindle that initial spark of empathy, effectively melting the frozen expanse of time between reader and ice-man.

Another favourite luring device of Riordan's reminds me of that childhood prank in which one friend clutches another after pretending to push him out into the passing traffic and says, "Saved yer life!". The longer poems here make a habit of throwing the reader gently off balance by dropping in some abstruse detail or other and then playing the hero by clarifying it some time later. Early on in 'The Sloe', for example, we learn that the ice-man "carried about him / not only weapons and tools / but spares, medicine, and a sewing kit, / fire and the means of fire". He carried fire? How on earth did he manage that? Fifteen lines later we learn that his equipment included a birch-bark container "insulated with damp sycamore leaves / (but no longer carrying live embers)".

But it's only in a poem of some length that Riordan is able to pull off this trick, and it's a trick that suits his writing very well. In some of the shorter poems you occasionally get the sense that their closure has come too soon – before their various elements have been properly resolved.

The collection is all the stronger, then, for being built around four long set pieces (between a hundred and two hundred and fifty lines long) which are placed like cornerstones at regular intervals throughout the book. My favourite of these, 'The Boy Turned into a Stag', is a version of a poem written by the Hungarian poet Ferenc Juhász and much admired by Auden. In it, time and order are once again knocked askew as a mother stands at her farmhouse door and calls to her grown-up son to come home to her for, she claims:

I have gone blind in this world of surfaces.
My shins are scarred, my eyes are bruised green-and-
                                                    yellow.
The universe rushes at me from all sides: the chair-leg,
the gatepost butt me with their horns; doors and
                                              windows jam,
the electric kettle shoots me with its volts; my
                                            sewing scissors
scuttle off my lap, the matches hop like wagtails' feet;
the pail handle nips at me like a cornered rat.

In her son's absence – or rather because of his absence – the mother's world has degenerated into a state of anarchy, and almost without our noticing the poem succeeds in catching us up in her unbridled angst. In the midst of the confusion a clutter of domestic paraphernalia becomes a menagerie of hostile creatures; it is almost as if, standing next to the mother, we feel ourselves rushed at, butted, nipped and shot with volts.

This poem, like several others in Maurice Riordan's Whitbread-nominated second collection, succeeds in doing what a good novel does: it manages to immerse us in a separate reality where "nature loses its solid manifestation. / And the world pauses" ('Floods'). That, for me, is the book's most impressive achievement.

ELAINE FEINSTEIN

Nigel Sutton

Elaine Feinstein has always been immersed in European and American poetry. Tsvetaeva is largely known to us through her piercing translations, and the range of her sympathies shows in her work, which is emotionally direct and, in her shorter poems, plangent. Her most recent book *Gold* (Carcanet, 2000) centres on the long title poem which brings her fictional and biographical skills into her poetry (She is currently writing a biography of Ted Hughes) in an exploration of the life of Leonardo da Ponte, Mozart's librettist. Her recent poetry is under no illusions about the status of the human animal: "Who set up Uncle Jo's Gulag / or sent Emma Lazarus's children off / to napalm gooks across Vietnam. / We did it. *Bong*. The human ape, / inheritor of the planet earth, and / from our power there's no escape".

from HOTEL MAIMONIDES

1

Bewildered in the glories of abundance,
imagine how our dead poets and scholars
would thread the chic streets of this Jewish quarter
and ask where is the scabrous past, the birdcages
the women in black clothes carrying herbs,
to Christian fires. After five centuries

the names on this square are of refugees
who took their skills away to Syria,
their languages, their medicine, their patience
and now by the great Mosque of Cordova
where jewellers sell rings of garnets in silver
they wander invisibly among tourists

puzzled to learn a Hebrew ancestor
is now more prized than limpieza de sangre.
In Spain, they love our ghosts. And we
who relish heaped fruits, a sleep post lunch
and sweet melocoton in this hotel
so grandly named after Maimonides

remain perplexed for all his guidance.
What will become of you now, my people
who returned from the Yemen on a white bird
that dropped out of the sky, or from their
scattering across North Africa and Uzbekistan
to claim a homeland? The history is not encouraging.

2

At home in Belsize Park as I wake to
the lark and the wren at 4 am and marvel
at the poise of birch trees after winter rain,
while the fresh leaves shiver in the subtle
grey light. I am disturbed
by another question:

What has the fanatic Middle East
to do with me? My grandparents
are buried in British earth, my children
are married out, my newspapers
concerned for the oppressed in camps, my synagogue
in dialogue with Said and Ashrawi.

Why are my dreams disturbed
by crossing borders, hiding, stories
of angry peasants and sly priests
when I look over a quiet garden
lit with pale sunshine? It is because
I have lived in a rare island of peace

where it is far too easy to be liberal
with desperate terrain for the dispossessed.
Over there, a secular embattled people
stubbornly defend a coastal strip, with
settlements and compromise no longer the issue,
uncertain the world accords them the right to exist.

CHARLES BOYLE

Richard Whitelaw

Charles Boyle's poetry evinces a very French kind of disaffection; he is,
says, Michael Hulse, "a connoisseur of dis-ease (Raymond Carver's
coinage), a grand master of the intuitions". Stendhal is explicitly his
mentor and many recent poems have epigraphs from that author.
Bilious, sardonic, he strikes a note of almost Brodskyish self-undramati-
zation in 'A Certain Age' from *Paleface* (Faber, 1996): "...friends, I say,
Romans, I'm a man, / I've been around if not far, I can hum a few tunes,
/ my patience is finite. I swing my arms as I walk". Several books from
Carcanet preceded *Paleface*, but there is no doubt that he has found his
true voice relatively late and that he has hit a richly entertaining seam.
His new collection, *The Age of Cardboard and String* (Faber, 2001), is
reviewed on p.45.

IN THE TOWN OF X

*When I arrive in a town I always ask: 1. Who are the twelve prettiest
women? 2. Who are the twelve richest men? 3. Which man could have
me hanged?*   Stendhal, *Souvenirs d'Egotisme*

The apprentice stylist, wiping the mirrors
in the empty salon,
then inspecting her gums;

the sisters in the orchard;
their seasoned mother; the outspoken
librarian, biting her lip through the day;

the homesick exchange student,
her reddened eyes and perfect shrug;
the miscast Lady Macbeth,
chain-smoking in the green room;

the cardinal's daughter;
the dental hygienist with flu;
the undertaker's widow;

and the woman in Zeno's pâtisserie
like the woman in that painting by Manet
behind the bar, bored
by the whiskers and paintbrushes of men –

little shivers of happiness
as one by one each places her hand
on the bevel of my hip,

while the chief of police
and eleven other rich men
jangling their keys, ordering more brandy,
avert their eyes.

*

Rainy afternoons,
we trail through the furniture emporium:
so much chrome, veneer and lacquer
gives us a headache, we want to lie down . . .

Or we take in a matinee at the temperance hall
by The Man Who Has All The Answers:
patient and exact, he fields every question
as if no one has asked it before.

The sky afterwards is overwhelmingly bright –
like matrimony, like just having bought something
you've saved up for for years,
or a stage-set for an execution.

Autumn Issue – Journeys

Wislawa Szymborska: new poems
Edwin Morgan interviewed
Mark Halliday on August Kleinzahler
Rod Mengham on Craig Raine
John Redmond on James Fenton

Published Oct 1 for National Poetry Day

His Teasing Ways

by James Keery

CHARLES BOYLE
The Age of Cardboard and String
Faber £7.99
ISBN 0571 206670

A POETIC MAGPIE, Charles Boyle has been "keeping a weather eye open / for the humdrum but telling detail" for so long that he was sure to recognise it if he ever found one. So far, he has had to make do with such delicacies as "these grey bits … in my seafood salad" ('Monday', *Paleface*, 1996), but at last, for his sixth collection, he has snapped up a gem. 'The Wellington Group' begins unprepossessingly with the longest and driest of a dozen epigraphs:

> The term refers to a loose association of New
> Zealand poets in Wellington, in the years between
> 1950 and 1965 … Certainly James K Baxter and
> Louis Johnson, both Wellington residents during the
> period, seemed to draw a number of poets around
> them: Alastair Campbell, for example, and the immi-
> grants Peter Bland and Charles Boyle.

> *The Oxford Companion to Twentieth Century Poetry*

"Remind me, Peter …": the deadpan opening line did the trick, and I'm still laughing. At the risk of revealing the cut of my anorak, I couldn't resist checking, and not only is the entry word for word, but there is a cross-reference between "Charles *Boyle" and "Boyle, Charles (1951-)":

> did I really sleep with Miss South Island
> '63, or was that something else

> I made up for the cv? But sometimes, Peter,
> after lunch with my agent

> in a restaurant where not even the cloakroom
>   attendant
> pretends he knows me, I'm there again . . .

> where James K Baxter holds me on his knee.
> I am four years old. I don't want to go to bed.

The joke's on Ian *Hamilton, "editor of this *Companion*", which offers "endless delightful knowledge to all poetry readers" (*Observer*), and, ironically, amongst the more painful influences on *Boyle's early verse (e.g. 'Cured', *Affinities*, 1977); on the unwary reviewer, who might, for example, describe Gael *Turnbull as a Canadian citizen, and in fact did, drawing a courteous rebuke from the poet for my pains; on Charles Doyle (genuine New Zealand poet, according to the superfluous 'Notes and Asides'); and also, of course, on *Boyle himself, who nevertheless takes particular pleasure in such one-letter-out misprints, or "Literals".

The sequence under that title features three more *trouvailles*. I wouldn't begrudge a subscription to Readers' Digest for "streets-weepers", but is "the horse in which Henry James was born" really worth a poem? "Howlingly funny", Sean *O'Brien? Are you sure? It is, however, around another intriguing "literal" that the collection coheres, though I admit that this time the penny *didn't* drop, until I got that irritating nudge. Perhaps *Boyle has given up waiting for readers to see the joke of his identification with Stendahl, which extends back through *Paleface*, his previous Faber collection, to 'Frog Prince', one of his contributions to *The New Poetry* (1993), written, at a guess, when he would have been, let me see now …

> at the age of thirty-eight – "the age when",
> as Stendahl himself remarks, "if one is disillusioned,
> boredom begins to appear on the horizon"…

One of the last poems, 'The Lady with the Dog' features an epigraph from *Souvenirs d'Egotisme* (neatly pre-empting *that* line of attack), in which Stendahl is accosted in London as "Mister Bell!" Just to make sure, "she insisted upon it, she knew my teasing ways, I was Beyle, Henri Beyle, also known as Stendahl". *Ah*, Beyle-Boyle, right, *with* you! "Beyle, I knew, though not a handsome man, was not without whatever it is to which women respond with that mixture of lust and ..." whatever. You and your "teasing ways", Charles, you *rake*, you!

In the epigraph to the book, from *La Chartreuse de Parme*, chapter 21, the Duchess expresses astonishment that "one of the greatest poets of the age" should be a thief, and in the first poem, 'A Respectable Neighbourhood', "a copy of *La Chartreuse de Parme*" falls open at guess which chapter? Mirror on mirror mirrored is all the show.

'Seven Poems from Prose by Stendahl' and 'Follain's Leeds' refract the poet's native city through the experience of the frog princes, but all that results is heartless cleverness: "the abbe's bloated / drifting corpse / becomes snagged on the piano stool"; "I hunker back to bed / to lick my beloved's nipples // while she reads aloud from 'The Work of Art / in the Age of Mechanical Reproduction'". Shame. Part of the charm of 'The Wellington Group' is its hint of nostalgia for a provincial literary scene, but *Boyle's city is the charmless destination of *Larkin's "salesmen" ('Friday Night in the Royal Station Hotel'). Yet "Follain's Leeds" is also *Paulin's, and notable poetic rhubarbarians include *Harrison, *Silkin, *Heath-Stubbs and *Hill, as well as the Apocalyptics, J F *Hendry, Dorian Cooke and Keidrych Rhys, who passed himself off as Dylan *Thomas to obtain drinks in local pubs; and Barry Tebb, whose wonderful day-glo Sixties Press productions keep the Apocalyptic flame alive.

"Who does he think he is? – latecomers / may wonder", but the anxious latecomer in 'Summer School', 'The Marquis de la Mole' himself, is rather obviously none other than *Boyle. 'The Body Double' continues the theme of being "almost" the real thing that *Boyle knows he isn't. Or not often. The title poem attributes all his poems to 'Mechanical Reproduction', but the glumness is delightfully sent up:

> It is a machine for eating oranges …
> It is a rocket bound for the moon.
> It is, whichever string you pull, the same machine.
>
> When it breaks we apply more sellotape,
> and when it breaks again we sulk, mixing our tears
> into the glue. When it works,
>
> we set off for the moon,
> scattering orange peel on the floor …

Wallace and Grommet aren't far away, but rocket flares do look a little like twists of peel, and the creator of this particular contraption deserves the sun, the moon and the oranges.

LIZ LOCHHEAD

Liz Lochhead's theatre work has sometimes been more prominent than her poetry but she was in the forefront of the Scottish poetic Renaissance with poems like 'Bagpipe Muzak'. She is one of those poets who can translate dramatic performance gestures into phrases that work on the page and she can do brilliant set-pieces like 'Advice to Old Lovers ("Please, though, have the manners to refrain from anything too tastelessly *specific* / Do steer clear of anything that might embarrass / On your little light-and-laughing sorties down memory lane. / Don't remind her of that night on the hearthrug after 'Last Tango in Paris'"). *Bagpipe Muzak* (Penguin, 1991) is still her principal collection. A selection appeared alongside Roger McGough and Sharon Olds in *Penguin Modern Poets 4* (1995).

THE BAKER

I am as lucky for a funeral
As a sweep is at a wedding
When with his red eyes, furred brush and burnt smell
He blesses bridal lace with his soil and smirching.

Thus do my work-night whites,
The cracks on my dusted boots,
My overall trousers of flour-stiffened linen
Handsel your black ties and pressed mourning suits

Although I am not by your side, nor
Does any one photograph my – or that rawest – absence.
Dawn delivery to this hotel had me
Shoulder those boards of my generous dozens

As all week neighbours came with bakestuffs
Up the saddest path to your door
Wanting to bring something sweet and light
To where nothing can be so any more.

And now I sleep on sacks washed soft
While you – your time at the cold grave over,
Or after that stare at the core of the terrible oven –
Take tea and funeral cakes together.

Let sober girls in black and white replenish plates
And freshen up the cooling cups with warm
As if tomorrow like live yeast could rise and prove.
I say: such crumbs do no harm.

In nights while I will work and you will grieve
Weak tea, sudden hunger for the heel of a new loaf,
White dawn and the surprise of appetite
Will have you tear a lump of goodness off.

Sooner, later a new season's wind will lift –
Though it may be many daily loaves from this dark hour –
As you let go, fling, and feel the ashes sift
Around your footsteps like spilt flour.

JOHN FULLER

Charles Hopkinson

John Fuller's reputation was to some extent sidelined in the 'eighties with the rise of provincial poets who were often explicitly anti-Oxford. But Fuller's poetry is some of the most inventive and graceful to appear in English in the late 20th century, and if invention and grace are deprecated that is an indictment of the times not the poetry. In any case, his *Collected Poems* (Chatto, 1996) led to a reappraisal: Sean O'Brien said: "Even the most suspicious critic is likely to be drawn back to the habitual brilliance of Fuller's technique, allied as it is with an imagination that begins where most others would leave off". In his most recent work, a strong humanistic civic note has emerged in poems concerned with the current state of the world. The long poem 'Europe' from *Stones and Fires* (Chatto, 1996) is an Audenesque meditation on European history with the Bosnian war in mind: "To be the powers! To sit with microphones / At tables gently circular as the / Great Globe itself, speaking aloud from thrones / Disguised as sofas..."

STREET LANGUAGE

1. PIGEONS IN BALHAM HIGH ROAD

This is what you wanted, and what you lean
Out to see from your pushchair: the pigeons
Hunched in the feathered ruffs of their grey greatcoats.

What is it you find to say about these old soldiers?
Is it the startling rise and flutter of broken wings
Above their waddling interest in scraps, the stoical hoarding

And release of rivalrous impulses, that intrigues you?
They are not beautiful, these exiles, but they strike
The attitudes still of their feathered and aerial kind.

Simply they are pavement birds, of the gutter
And fending life. Their memory of exploit
Is like your intuition of its possibility.

For you murmur over their names in your own way,
Your own babble and cooing, that knows what it is
To be so privileged in life as to have such a great idea of it.

2. FUCHSIA

What does the flower say, which you have learned to touch
Without tearing, cupping it briefly beneath the chin?
Its bright lips seem to open in wonder, like your own.

You are held up to it, as to the light of a lantern,
And light is all it needs, the adjectival voice of colour,
Repetitive, exclamatory, and at the same time silent.

The garden is red at the ends, as though it had been dipped,
Red and magenta, like the bells of a jester.
It bursts into its still and soundless frenzy.

In this fragrant room without a ceiling, water is trickling
And you are eager again to strangle the green snake.
Yours will be the human language of busy verbs.

The grass is crawling with its own little phrases of wings and legs.
The air is full of the flag telegraphy of butterflies.
What does the flower say? Bffzz-tszz-zng-btzzzzz . . .

3. DA

What will the first word be, Daddy or Dog?
Neither are wholly benign, like nursery Nana,
Nor wholly disgraceful, like kennelled Mr Darling.

They are both words you can hammer your tongue under.
Da, you say. Oh! Da, is what it says, too.
Da, you say. It is both a self-touching and a projection.

Like all language, you feel it between your head
And the world that rolls unendingly before you
As you chase across the rug, slapping it out of the way.

While you are crawling, you can pretend to be the dog
Who fascinates you. But surely preference must be given
To the tall Da who makes you fly? A puzzle!

Down from the ceiling, twisting to get to the rug again
To be that rough one, you briefly brush the mouth that is like yours.
Now, think of all the words you can say standing up.

4. RADIO BABY

Beneath the eaves they are talking to their mothers
And their mothers are talking, too, with pacifying voices
Over systems of alarm that accidentally connect

Speaker to speaker, from nursery to bedroom
And from house to house, the length of Tunley Road.
What can a baby have to say to a mother who is not his own?

It's a busy wavelength that will blur like this,
Thinner than an eyelash darkened with tears.
It is the kinship of blood, like a year of fine wines.

But a mother knows the voiceprint of her own child,
Knows it in utter darkness, in her sleep of remembered maidenhood,
In the silence of communication and in the chatter of dawn.

This is Radio Baby you are tuned to, Radio Baby!
With all its regular programmes, its clatter and announcements.
Its easy quizzes. The laughter. The audience participation.

5. DRUMS AT THE TOOTING DURBAR

M'Lord's carriage has stalled in the grass, in the commons.
Shall there be dancing to entertain him?
Shall they entertain him, the dainty kings and queens?

What's this, a dog? Oh! Oh! But it's unbelievable!
The freedom, the roughness of utterance! And the colours in the sky.
The strolling in no direction. The sizzling sweetmeats.

What is the difference between a drum and a balloon?
A balloon is large enough to head-butt through the grass
At the pace of a controlled scamper. A drum is a sound.

The drums speak the language of a nodding procession,
Hips turning, fingers pointing, fingers fat with rings,
Whole bodies edging along, half queue, half conga.

The drums speak the language of golden crowns,
Bent knuckles on the skin, dabbling the cheeks of the drum,
The sound filling the fragrant afternoon like a fountain.

SUSAN WICKS

New Generation was quite good at selecting poets who confounded its press releases, i.e. were not working class, media savvy, streetwise poets. Many of them were *sui generis* and none more so than Susan Wicks. Her poetic models are French and American rather than English. She studied French literature, wrote a thesis on André Gide, and her cited influences at the time of New Generation were Apollinaire, Gerald Stern and Sharon Olds. She has been highly productive since 1994, writing two novels, a prose memoir and a third collection, *The Clever Daughter* (Faber, 1997). Many of the poems in *The Clever Daughter* are about the death of her parents. It is a sombre volume, pervaded by swirling dark currents. When she writes of spring she is even bleaker than Larkin: "How can we live with green, / this ache of trees, this perennial reading / into light, the air that dances?"

Joanna Eldredge Morrissey

PAINT

Not just the reek of paint,
his brush sliding and stroking
the grain of the open window,
the frame where I could see myself
as a pale shadow

but that warm stink of my own
that rose to meet his high gloss
as I tensed and listened
for his feet across the roof-tiles,
his rhythmic hiss.

Inside that sick marriage
of smells, a green satin salon
under clear plastic, Spirou, Asterix,
a corridor skating-rink,
terrapins fogged in their dark tank.

And at our feet, Paris, its star
of cars, metallic silk
threading the lined-up arches,
where children with dark socks
played by cement basins, on gravel walks.

Behind me, a sudden laugh.
He is an acrobat
jumping from roof to roof.
His grin flashes through glass
as he waves his dripping brush.

This shadow at my back
could lean out, spatter a whole town
with pale green paint, or step off
into nothing. He hums as he works.
And me with my knickers down.

LEAVING

What they are saying could be anything,
the shreds of oily green
carried to their mouths, tines flashing,
faces captive in the bowls of spoons.

Wine shivers. On their knees
napkins with the folds still in them.
Outside, the night river
exposes its liquid tongues.

Beached plastic bottles, the dark hulls
of tethered barges – until
a phone rings, a knife falls
in a smeared zigzag of oil

as she throws back her chair. The men
talk among themselves, the rich food
divided between them, the river
lost behind glass – for all she knows

the tide has turned, the lights are blinking out,
the bottles lift and float,
the barges shudder, pulling
on other ropes, as the salt water

floods back. She hasn't said
goodbye. Whatever has called her –
sick child, fire, death, a cat
in a blood and mucous mess

of crushed bone – she's leaving,
letting the men talk on,
the ordered courses mounting at her back
– not caring if she's forgiven.

JAMES LASDUN

Lasdun is better known as a short story writer than a poet, perhaps because he lives in New York and is therefore off the circuit, perhaps because his work is stylistically unfashionable. Lasdun's prose has received the highest praise from the notoriously hard to please James Wood: "Lasdun seems to be one of the secret gardens of English writing... when we read him we know what language is for". But Lasdun is also a poet's poet, and the most gifted of the younger poets writing in a vein that could be called Hechtian. Indeed, it is pleasing that the master himself has recognised this, writing on the back cover of his latest collection: "Brilliant... full of linguistic panache, uncommon depths of feeling, fine ironies, and taut drama". This vein involves a dazzling descriptive technique, using quite subtle metaphysics, and the subject matter is often decadent. At its best the sheer physical charge of poems like 'On the Road to Chenonceaux', or 'Buying a Dress' is exhilarating. Lasdun's new collection, his third (reviewed on p.54), chronicles his move to upstate New York and his adoption of a homesteading life.

BLACK LOCUST GROVE

For Jonathan Nossiter

Shallow-rooted like us,
less colonists than refugees,
they crowd into spent farmland,
twisting to find the light,
eking out thin livings; ghetto trees,

branchless till they crown, sparsely;
all thrift against the summer foliage,
swaying in ghostlike plumes as if our grave
forefathers had come back to observe us
working beneath them on the porch.

Named for a desert scourge
their pods are said to resemble,
they press their kinship through our own names;
our strangeness in the Anglo-Saxon forest
of Smiths and Browns ours clashed with every roll-call.

(Homework: invent your family's crest;
maybe you never had to but I did:
a dun-colored lass – what else? The class tittered.
Later I invented my family's psychology:
Anglo, Super-Anglo and Yid.)

A diet of dust and stones. But that's behind us,
isn't it? Sweetened to milk and honey . . .
Though whatever complicity
we aspire to with these black locusts,
it isn't that their leaves turn out to be money,

but their pure obduracy, their rock-smooth
rings like agate rings, so hard the wood
won't rot or even soften when it's dead
but sparks against the chainsaw blade
and burns too hot for comfort in the woodstove.

ADAM

Seed-hoarder: tipping his paper pouches
in unnibbleable coffers; fencing,
filching our food, homeland; won't chatter
the local woods brogue of chirrup and chuck.
his othering tongue unchristening tree,
unrocking rock.

He's not one of us; he's
definitely not one of us:
unstriped meat-breather pissing ammonia; we feign
blitheness but from each
brush-pile, oak-stump, ash-limb,
we are watching him.

Blades in the Catskills

by Douglas Houston

JAMES LASDUN

Landscape with Chainsaw

Cape, £8.00
ISBN 0 224 06107 0

LANDSCAPE WITH CHAINSAW is uneven, though its triumphs ensure overall success. Such admirable poems as 'The Apostate', 'Hops', and 'Woodstock'

are peaks in the collection's sustained meditation on belonging and deracination. The landscape of the title is that of the Catskill Mountains, New York State, where a confrontation with the imperatives of survival gives urgency to the poetry's re-negotiation of identity. Translated from his uneasy place in the British middle-classes as one of a family of "anglophone Russian-German apostate Jews", Lasdun embraces life in the wilds on the same terms as his immigrant predecessors:

> . . . Being here's just a question of having been
> Elsewhere unhappily long enough to feel
> That that was exile, this not.

> ('American Mountain')

The gift of a chainsaw initiates the rite-ofpassage between the inauthenticities of the former existence and the winning of a sense of belonging on the mountainside. 'Returning the Gift' follows the poet's responses on acquiring the chainsaw. Misgivings concerning its lethal potential are displaced by a backwoods salesman, whose homily of encouragement draws on the precepts of pioneer masculinity in Robert Bly's 'Iron John'. Subsequent poems celebrate new intensities of lyricism discovered in the act of using the chainsaw, revitalising the cliché in "the need to carve out a niche for ourselves" with vividly literal meaning:

> And if song is existence,
> One could do worse for the roar
> Of life being lived to the hilt
> Than a blade plunged in solid wood.
>
> ('Chainsaw II')

Lasdun's existential re-location is reflected in the stylistic accommodation between the strictly regulated forms of his European inheritance and the freer, more conversationally direct, verse idioms native to his American environment. There's a loose-limbed spaciousness about much of the writing, which sits well with the exploratory impulse seeking to define the character of this *vita nuova* in the Catskills. Rhyme is frequently used, though with a licence which admits anything between full chimes and the merest ghost of a correspondence. 'American Mountain', for example, follows its ABCB pattern with complete pairings like "masses / classes" and strong half-rhymes like "home / claim", only to lose the plot with such conjunctions as "lopped / Jews" or "hole / lungs". The poem, it seems, has more important business than contriving a better-regulated music. Elsewhere, notably in 'The Backhoe' and 'Property: the Bear', Lasdun sustains intricate rhyme schemes with impressive consistency.

The book displays a similarly arbitrary tendency to de-regulation in the recurrence of *ad hoc* hyphenated compounds. Examples are "grandfather-in" (p. 4) , "money-soul" (p.18), and "bee-balm" (p. 30). This can amount to an irritating tic, as can the ready recourse to such neologistic constructions as "unnibbleable" (p. 7), "othering tongue unchristening tree" (ibid.), "Judasless" (p. 27), and "mammaly" (p. 8) – (why not "mammalian", or, in context, "mammary" ?).

Poems of personal retrospection are among the most striking. 'The Apostate' and 'Hops' contain lyrically opulent treatments of Englishness. The former deals with Lasdun's mother and her strained endeavours to erase the differences between her immigrant Jewish self and her English environment by joining the Anglican Church:

> Out in the jangling air
>
> She feels invisible, dispersed,
> As if the gold-lipped chalice
> Had swallowed her into itself;
> Into the iron and flagstones, the pitted pillars,
> Into the earth outside – and this is grace,
>
> briefly.

'Hops' moves seamlessly from the remembered sting of an insult in an English pub through a luminous sequence on a summer spent hop-gathering to its concluding burst of Catskills lyricism. A transatlantic perspective encompasses both the realities of alienation and the emblematically vivid mythos of Englishness, the "Albion juju" whose spell confers its deceptive sense of belonging.

Command of such imaginative range and fluency of modulation underlie the outstanding success of 'Woodstock', the thirty-one stanza penultimate poem. Prep-school and its polymorphous eroticism, Arthurian legend, the Woodstock festival, and Lasdun's memories of sustaining a severe injury are masterfully conflated. Once again, the present-tense of the Catskill Mountains supplies a vantage point from which these motifs are brought together in a single imaginative field of vision. As a speedboat's propeller slashes his arm, the moment of beholding "the unsheathed sword of my own / startlingly white bone" gains shocking impact from its alignment with images of Excalibur rising from the water and Jimi Hendrix raising his guitar aloft at the festival.

Landscape with Chainsaw has a great deal to recommend it, not least its occasional touches of dry humour:

> I invented my family's psychology:
> Anglo, Super-Anglo and Yid

It'll be interesting to see how life and art go on in the Catskills in his next collection.

ROBYN BOLAM

Robyn Bolam's two collections of poetry, *The Peepshow Girl* (Bloodaxe, 1989) and *Raiding the Border* (Bloodaxe, 1996), were published under her married name, Marion Lomax. When divorce followed bereavement and illness, she changed her name last year to make a new start. In her first two books, her Northumbrian background was to the fore in many of the poems. In *Raiding the Border* she teases away at the betwixt and between nature of land that was alternately claimed by England and Scotland: "England was never an only child, / but has grown to think so". Her poems are painterly in their descriptions and the poems of relationships oblique and taut with significance. She also writes in other voices: from Eurydice to a Northumbrian housewife's characteristic natter.

TWO SPRINGS

One north is not like another: one flight
north by northeast – under two hours
and I'm plunged back into winter;
snow still patches the dead ground.
The thermometer outside my window
reads two degrees when I mist the glass.

I know there are bluebells in England:
days ago, I walked through them
in a leafy wood. Here, trees are too bare
to imagine leaves – and the only blue
is a ship in the harbour, bigger than
millions of bluebells, blocking out a church
and a run of roofs with its cold bulk –
booming in the night, like a restless animal
taking soundings off Finland or Estonia.

Now we have rain from a grey sky
and the figures on the walkway,
half-way up a hillside, hurry,
walk stiffly, their eyes on the ground,
as if, by staring, they will warm it
and make the grass grow.

I live in eight tiers of single people,
draw the blinds when they do,
turn up the heat, boil a pot
on the stove to make some tea.
The radio tells me there are wolves

still – in Sweden. When the ship
booms again, I think I can hear them
calling down from the north
that winter is ending.

CACTI AND LOVE

I knew the desert without driving to it:
the road went straight through my forehead.
Fat branch stumps of Joshua trees,
like a cross between a cactus and a palm,
stopped a long way short of the clear deep sky.

Cacti reminded me of my mother –
difficult to touch without injury to each other.
But when she was happy, relaxed, no tensions,
her smiles were exotic, unexpected flowers.
Her cacti bear with me and still blossom.

We both needed love: I still need it now,
and hope is everywhere in a desert –
cacti bloom; light lifts us into its space.
We forget alien distance, the lack of water:
cacti and love outlive their owners.

COLETTE BRYCE

Joe Bulaitis

Colette Bryce's debut volume *The Heel of Bernadette* (Picador, 2000) announced the arrival of an unusually gifted poet. She comes from Derry and is brilliant at registering the shock of events ("the crack of its bones chilled my own. / I sank another, severed the neck"). She has fine rhythmic control over rhymed stanzas and the movement of her poems is sometimes reminiscent of Simon Armitage: "I have never met anyone with such keen ears / as the man from Moville who soberly swears / on each loose leaf of his family tree / (as traced to the deep armada wreck / by the aunt who famously leased the shack..."). She is good at those long perspectives Larkin was terrified of: in 'Nevers' she writes of "Passions never spoken, / never broken, but preserved, / never layered under marriages / or burnt to dust by fast affairs". And the future? "we harbour it in our hearts / like a terrible crush. We laugh / and drink to this in rented rooms. //We think Not this, but older, elsewhere, soon" ('Hit Shite and it Flies High'). *The Heel of Bernadette* was an ultra slim volume but it was well worth getting these poems into circulation. The next will be more than usually eagerly awaited.

STONES

We kept ourselves from children who were rich,
who were shaped in the folds of newest clothes,
who were strapped in the backs of foreign cars
whose quick electric windows rose
effortlessly, that poured into the stream of traffic;

but stared, fascinated, at their orthodontic
iron smiles, their nerve averted eyes.

They were quiet. They feared rain. They were taught
to recite in yellow rooms *Colette, Suzette,*
Jo-jo and Lou are coming here for tea . . .
or to sing from the prompt of a tuning fork
How merry your life must be. . .

They had no idea, but disappeared
to the South of France twice a year –
as we ran the streets, the lanes and squares,
robbers, outlaws, ne'er-do-wells –
then left for schools we didn't know.

From walls we saw them come and go.
War-daubed faces, feathers in our hair, wild,

we never smiled.

THE WORD

He arrived, confused, in groups at the harbours,
walking unsteadily over the gangways;
turned up at airports, lost in the corridors,
shunted and shoved from Control to Security;
fell, blinking and bent, a live cargo
spilled from the darks of our lorries,
dirty looking, disarranged, full of lies, lies,
full of wild stories, *threats and guns and foreign wars*
or He simply appeared, as out of the ground,
as man, woman, infant, child, darkening doorways,
tugging at sleeves with *Lady, Mister, please,*
please . . .

There were incidents; He would ask for it
with His crazy gestures, rapid babble, swaying
His way through rush hour trains, touching people,
causing trouble, peddling guilt in the market place,
His thousand hands demanding change, flocking
in rags to the steps of the church, milking
the faithful, blocking the porch, He was chased –
but arrived in greater numbers, needs misspelt
on scraps of paper, hungry, pushy, shifty, gypsy,
not comprehending *No* for an answer. What could we do?
We turned to the word. We called to our journalists,
they heard

and hammered a word through the palms of His hands, SCAM.
They battered a word through the bones of His feet, CHEAT.
Blood from a bogus crown trickled down, ran
into His eyes and His mouth and His throat, OUT.
He gagged, but wouldn't leave.
We rounded Him up with riot police,
drove Him in vanloads out of our streets,
away from our cities, into the tomb
and slammed the door on a job well done.
We are safer now, for things have changed:
we have laws in place like a huge, immovable stone,

should He rise again.

HARRY CLIFTON

Pat McGuigan

Harry Clifton early on adopted a fairly common strategy for Irish poets – to live abroad. His work in places as diverse as Vietnam, the Abruzzi mountains in Italy, and Paris where he now lives, has given him a perspective rare in contemporary poetry but has also, perhaps, restricted his readership. Most of his books have been published by Gallery in Ireland with the exception of a very slim Bloodaxe selected poems, *The Desert Route*, in 1992. Clifton began as a follower of Derek Mahon, and his poetry has gained in power in recent years. In poems like 'Taking the Waters' a sensibility that will become more common in time is on display: that of a world citizen (or at least predominantly European), in the conventional sense rootless, but rooted in what Mikhail Gorbachev once wistfully called "our common European home". Clifton's urban cultural reveries convey the excitement and loneliness of city life better than anybody else now writing. His prose book *On the Spine of Italy* (Pan, 2000) has been widely admired and sold well; his reviewing is exemplary; it is time his poetry had equal recognition. His latest collection is *Night Train through the Brenner* (Gallery, 1994).

READING SAINT AUGUSTINE

Huge stanzas, on the end of the world,
Were crowding in like weather, scudding cloud
And changing light, on Monday the twenty-third
At the breakfast table. Light of heart
And casual, with the working week ahead,
We went to our rooms. Again, the traffic noise
Outside my window. Quieter, outside yours,
A garden, finches, at the back of the house.
And this we called our discipline, our art,
Internal, focussed, warding off the powers
Of dissolution, each in our own small way,
Ideal or real, sufficient unto the day.

As for myself, I was desperate to get back –
That sacred book, Augustine's *City of God* –
To a time behind our time, of plunder and sack,
Where the word Apocalypse was clearly stated.
Better not to write then, just to read –
To read and listen, only to bring in later
Everyday life, the baker up at four
Around the corner, six months from retirement
And his millionth loaf, the silence of mid-morning
On every floor, the boy delivering fliers,
The postgirl with her sad impetigoed face,
When the Beginning and End were definitely in place.

As for yourself, I hesitate to speak –
Doing it better than I, whatever you did –
With your pregnant myth, expanding by the hour,
Incorporating gardens into the Garden,
Burrowing into consciousness and id,
Abandoning Logos, cultivating Psyche,
Plot and character, what the butler saw
Of more than manners – in a word, real life,
For what did anyone know of Eternal Law?
Bypassing the Sublime for someone's grief,
Irrational, undignified, humanly true,
Staying faithful only to what you knew.

Eleven thirty. Carthage and Thagaste
Long since fallen, knew their gods had failed.
Alaric and his Huns had stove them in
Like Rome before them. Adeodatus the bastard
Of Augustine, and Augustine himself, were dead.
All that was left, now, was the *City of God.*
The orgies, the pomaded boys, the love-ins,
All were over. Outside, sirens wailed –
A truck rolled by, the windowglass vibrated.
Otherwise, all was normal. In your room
Another sentence formed. *For even without him
Her life would go on.* I stood in the kitchen, waited

For coffee to boil, and time to come to an end.
Monday, the day for maids. Behind the garden
Whiteclad women put their house in order.
One, who had just stayed over, ran her hands
Along her cheekbones, loving herself in a mirror,
Rubbing facecream in. A morning after –
Sinless, without guilt. Supernatural terror?
I could hear her hard, ironical laughter
Echoing through the ages, the sacked empires,
Back to Alaric. No, on the twenty-third,
For all its cloud-apocalypse funeral pyres,
Women, it seemed, would have the final word.

THE STREET OF THE FOUR WINDS

After the liquid lunches, the slippage and lost ground
Of so many cities, and trying to find our feet
On alien pavements, your lore and my lore,
Let's have another, and where do we go from here,
That well-known little-spoken-of discreet
Establishment on the Street of the Four Winds,

Open all day and night, its empty afternoons
For rent by the hour, will take us in,
No questions asked, the ghosts of others' honeymoons
Who have left their overnight bags and gone on the town.
And there the state of marriage and living in sin,
The one in the other, the bed of straw and the bed of down,

Will be given us to make love in, and doze
Till the chime of awakening, and the chambermaid's knock,
And whose are they anyway, these borrowed keys
To our own pure strangeness, on somebody else's sheets?
Whatever you do, don't go to the window and look
Or ask which year, which city. Four Winds Street –

An indigence, a dream of dining out
On the goodwill of millions, as they go about
Unconscious business, here or anywhere,
Letting us be. Above, the hangman's rope
Of a naked lightbulb, as you pin your hair.
A Gideon bible to swear by, and a cake of fragrant soap

Like a vade mecum, to be pocketed free and taken
Into the latening world, of goings-home,
Old marriages. Again they will come,
The honeymoon couples, full of all they have seen,
To look right through us, like a might-have-been
Or another life, in a room they have mistaken.

CAROLE SATYAMURTI

Diana Matar

Carole Satyamurti's poetry has deepened since her debut volume *Broken Moon* (Oxford Poets, 1987). She now seems able to tackle any subject: from a poem on the immortal cell line HeLa to the Bosnian War, from 'The Trial of Lyman Atkins' to 'The Smell of Sweat'. Her voice is always wise and considered: what she has to say is interesting and her technique always deft and economical. In all this, she is sometimes reminiscent of the Polish poet Wislawa Szymborska. She often manages to find the metaphor *juste* for a nebulous state, as in 'Striking Distance', her poem about the emergence of ethic hatred in the Balkans, in which the way the obsession takes roots is likened to the tongue as it "tries to limit a secret sore". In 'Leasehold' the experience of revisiting an old family house is captured exactly: "it wasn't home I longed for / but for a second reparative twist / at turning points, the chance to etch a different / mark in that gas-fumed hallway..." She is a poet who writes of common humanity ("to swallow disgust and breathe / deeply the air you share with everyone") with uncommon insight and grace. Her latest book is *Love and Variations* (Bloodaxe, 2000).

EXPLAINING ZERO SUM FROM THE SNOWDROP HOTEL

We have blind spots.
Five times at least I've asked you to explain parallax;
and you say "zero sum" is meaningless to you.

I've held out for this room, high in the Alps,
against Americans whose sleep, now, will toss uneasily
through the trundle and rumble of lorries – the main road;
and, beyond it, trains clanking in from Italy.
My gain = their loss; that's zero sum.

My window overhangs a river, high on meltwater.
whirling past under an agate sky. "Come *on*", it calls,
"let's have an argument!" and I could leap over the sill
to plunge and wrestle, lose myself in being overcome.

Or I could sing like the invisible blackbird
who, at evening, pitches his notes clear
across the water, until the song seems to draw
its phrases from the river's rush and welter.

If, with each new tune, the river lost energy,
became less abundant until it thinned to a trickle
while the blackbird voiced ever more opulent
torrents of sound – that would be zero sum.

Or if, by its acrobatics, by sheer verve, the river
so daunted and engulfed the bird's inventions
that his song became mere cheep and whistle –
that would be zero sum.

But the blackbird opens his throat, and his song
bubbles and chuckles with all the river that is in it;
and the song returns to the water such vibrations
that the river becomes infused by song,
embodying, in endless tumble to the sea,
that sound, and its own.

And this is not zero sum – this is gain and gain!

GIVE ME A PIECE OF YOUR MIND, FAT MAN

I want to feel my bones packed snug in their upholstery,
so nothing in the mirror will remind me of the graveyard.

Let my whole poundage shake with seismic laughter as yours does;
let my sex astonish people, since they somehow hadn't reckoned on it.

Show me how warm it is when small children and cats snuggle
in the mounds and folds that spread from north to south of you.

Let me be a constant surprise as you are, mesmerising with your
deep voice and your high voice, when people expect you to be a joke.

I'd like to sing out of the ampleness of my fat cheeks, my massive chest,
my glorious acoustic, to be a convincing hero against all tittering.

Let me give orders without apologetic fidgeting, wield calm
and incontestable authority. Let me be a walking lie detector.

I want to know your dolphin buoyancy in water, your understated
footwork on the dance floor, axle in a whirling dazzle of jive.

I'd hate to have to act impervious in restaurants, eat in the face
of all those mimsy appetites staring as though you had the pox,

but when you take your clothes off and strut in a sash, wrestle
huge weight balancing huge weight – I want to feel that,

to be made generous as a great bellied pot and, corpulent Gautama,
I want your staying power, your gravity, your far-seeing smile.

SARAH WARDLE

Sarah Wardle won *Poetry Review*'s Geoffrey Dearmer Prize in 1999. Her work is often light and playful, as in 'Poet's Parliament', here, but can be more serious. She has a foot in both the mainstream and light verse camps, a useful stance. A philosophical note pervades her work, a ripe field for light verse: ("You see it's the physical stuff I miss / Since the hemlock, I've put emphasis / on experience, not universals" – 'Socrates to Descartes'). She writes well about the experience of illness and beyond that her subject matter roams pretty much where it will: travel poems ('In the National Palace Museum, Taiwan'), historical judgement ('Hubris'), the trade ('Reading Room Requiem'). A selection of her work appears in *Anvil New Poets 3*, edited by Roddy Lumsden and Hamish Ironside (Anvil, 2001) – see review on p.107. A full first collection shouldn't be too far away.

EASTBOURNE

Each summer brought them out again,
like gulls along the beach,
to gaze on the horizon
at a future out of reach,
or watch the pleasure boat board
from an *in memoriam* bench,
along with the holiday horde
and its salt'n'vinegar stench.

Winter would keep them in,
though on a brighter day
they'd drive out for a spin,
or have grandchildren to stay,
but this December afternoon
they sleep tight in their graves,
and Christmas lights are up so soon
beside the ceaseless waves.

POETS' PARLIAMENT

Suppose poets stood for Parliament,
that they ran as Independent candidates,
canvassing streets on council estates
with poems printed on cards which said,
"Sorry you were out when I called".
Suppose they read in village halls
to one man and a dog. Suppose they formed a party
and romped home with a landslide victory,
that after the General Election,
their maiden speeches were their first collections.

Imagine they took their seats in the Chamber,
resting their feet on its benches' green leather,
whilst at the Dispatch Box the Junior Minister
for Sonnets held forth on the merits of metre,
as "Order! Word order!" – was called by the Speaker.
Imagine the Gallery full of Strangers,
recognising bards from Panorama,
or interviews held on College Lawn
about their favourite poems for the News at Ten.
Imagine poets' statues in Parliament Square
to Pope and Cope, or Ted and Sylvia.

Picture poets pacing the Committee Corridor,
composing a line instead of toeing one,
or seated at tables in the Tea Room alone,
scribbling on envelopes which bear the portcullis.
Picture them sipping Pimms on the Terrace,
with memos in verse circulating in Ministries,
along with rhymed soundbites on Government policies.
Picture poets of the past, now in the canon,
kicked up to the Lords, like Elysium,
as if the dead had wandered over
from across the road in Poets' Corner
to sit in ermine robes, day-dreaming,
still able to influence a Poem's First Reading.

And suppose that in Central Lobby the Saints
for England, Scotland, Ireland and Wales were replaced
with Dylan Thomas over one arch, above another Yeats,
over the third arch William Shakespeare,
and Burns above the last which leads to the bar.

PETER ARMSTRONG

Dominic Turner

Peter Armstrong's imagination is drawn to the bleak open spaces – firstly, of his native Northeast of England, and secondly, of a mythic mid-western America and its depiction in popular and folk song. It is powerful stuff, sensuous in a numbed, grit-scoured kind of way. He has tuned in to the powerful imagery of the blues. In this world you hear "the dying fall of a steel guitar", "the radio is teased to a V8 throb", and "just across the top of the hill / Maybelline may be waiting, / a seaboard, anything". He is expert at fusing the actual imagery of the bleak heart-land of America and the technology of recorded sound: "Beyond the four-shack city / and its LAST GAS BEFORE TUNDRA! / the road-signs bleach to nothing / or they label something final: / the little, the less, and the ice-line, / the hiss at the end of the vinyl". He has worked as a psychiatric nurse and cognitive therapist, and some of his eroded landscapes are those of the mind. His second collection, *The Red Funnelled Boat* was published by Picador in 1998.

GRYKE AND THE SOCRATIC METHOD

The tape whirs, or the striplight, or
the breathing of a guard becomes
everything that isn't some
tie between inquisitor

and the one who longs to tell.
(Telling now would be a Joy.)
Everything is miles away
– this room, a siren somewhere, all

that falls outside the circle of
your face, your arms, my arms, my face –
How long need we go on with this?
(How much have you the need to prove?)

The tape whirs, or the day outside
creeps up the avenues and revs
the engines on a million drives;
beyond the city limits ride

our visions of the interstates
– perspective-exercising roads
whose lonely fugitives are gods
that nobody interrogates.

ALISON BRACKENBURY

Veronica Jones

Alison Brackenbury doesn't fit any of the hand-me-down stylistic or generational labels currently available. She is a contemporary of Sean O'Brien and Andrew Motion but her work has always stood against any current. Unusually amongst modern poets she works in her family business, an electroplating firm, and this grounding appears attractively in some of her poems. When she writes of 'Bookkeeping', one is aware of how rarely work as a subject like this appears in modern poetry. Formally, she writes tightly metrical stanzas, often with a strong rhythmic whirl running though them. In fact, she proves that the traditional technique of emotional lyric poetry can still carry the charge it always has. She has also managed to continue to write about nature in an essentially urban age, investing it with a rare urgency: "It is not tall enough, it will not make a crop – / It has changed its name. It used to be flax..." ('Linum'). Her latest collection is *After Beethoven* (Carcanet,1999).

CRACKED

To watch the sewer on video
Is just to watch a white light crawl
Through tunnels with their quick grey flow,
Not horror, but the breath's sharp fall
As cameras skim the dripping walls,

A trick, a ride, the sluggish world
Which beats beneath these roads and grass
Where patient roots prise open welds
Small geysers blow, unseen, rats drink.
Then finally, the whole pipe sinks.

How happy are the engineers
Who type their black and clean report.
The sewer throbs beneath our ground.
Neighbours rush in. We must pay all!
A half – a sixth? A thousand pounds?

So did my roots claw out its heart?
"Claims leakage" the insurance man
Calls our grave hopes. Seams gape apart,
Night stains the day. White moths are seen
Whirling through the air above
The untrenched grass, so strangely green.

THE BLUE DOOR

The door swings slowly to one side.
As people cough before the play
A rectangle of blue light rides

Behind the stage. There's nothing there
But dust and cold, the little comb
Which slipped from the last dancer's hair

Which she will never see again:
The glow on dunes the child saw,
Sea's plain beyond, then the sky's pane

Above the lover's bed, the cry
Of day reflected back again:
A blue square in the baby's eye.

The light grows richer, stills then thins.
The dark is quiet. The play begins.

Stepping Stones

By Stephen Burt

EDNA LONGLEY

Poetry & Posterity

Bloodaxe, £10.95
ISBN 1 853224 435 6

EXAMINING POETS' RESPONSES to modern wars, and to Northern Ireland's Troubles, *Poetry in the Wars* (1986) established Edna Longley as a critic with whom to reckon. She's since emerged as a champion of relatively skeptical, self-conscious, and Horatian modern poets (especially Edward Thomas and Louis MacNeice) as against more ambitious, less ironic, and (not coincidentally) nationalist visions. Longley (who teaches at Queen's University, Belfast) has also become a caustic critic of (pseudo) literary and (quasi) politi-

cal assumptions, especially where they touch on things Irish: a poetry critic, but also a critic of culture, and a sometimes severe critic of critics. This fairly big, fairly academic book of recent essays confirms her in those strengths.

Longley's introduction invokes "the idea of posterity", which "is inseparable from the idea of value": Yeats liked to contemplate permanence, Frank O'Hara transience, but both writers matter to us (Longley suggests) because they made poems that last. Invoking "Irish poets' awareness of multiple audiences, multiple traditions", Longley promises to demonstrate "how poets take the chances that language gives them", and how they respond to what history brings. Such demonstrations come, for her, mostly in quarrels with other critics: most of Longley's essays are what my teachers in graduate school called "interventions", attempts to alter ongoing debates.

One such debate concerns "ecocentrism" – the newly (and understandably) fashionable way of reading which looks for Green concerns, and praises writers who show them. Longley finds "Green politics / poetics" in Edward Thomas, "not only conceptually but also in terms of poetic structure". His poetic "eco-history" lets him "search for other parameters in addition to class-politics": it may not have been easy being Green, but Thomas preferred it to turning Red. A long, admiring analysis of MacNeice's 'All Over Again' (not, for me, among his strongest poems), a neat discussion of Yeats's 'The Wild Swans at Coole', and a whole essay on Auden's 'In Praise of Limestone' discover Green attitudes in all three poets: Auden explores in his calcium carbonate landscape a "creative tension between the human artifact and the natural or historical forces that tend to 'dissolve' it". Longley's substantial 'Pastoral Theologies' turns on one big opposition: (1) truly eco-conscious writing, attentive to nature for its own sake (and therefore respectful of secular science) against (2) "animist" or crypto-Catholic pastoral. No prizes for guessing which one Longley prefers – or which one Seamus Heaney writes. Unlike Thomas, Heaney in *Field Work* "does not seek to express 'the earth'; he proposes… 'earth' as a metaphor for poetic expression". Fair enough, as description; odd, as a basis for judgement – must he "express the earth"? (If Longley is really trying to be a doctrinaire Green, she'll have to stop liking O'Hara, who "couldn't enjoy a blade of grass", he wrote, without "a subway or a record store handy".)

'Pastoral Theologies' links eco-Longley to her other big agenda: an attack on "versions of 'Irish poetry' [which] allow 'Irish' to usurp or subordinate 'poetry'". Such "ethno-criticism" (she objects) turns what should be readings of poems into readings and judgements of "England" and "Ireland". At a recent French festival, Longley writes, "Parisian intellectuals raved about *celtique* spirituality, while Irish writers objected coarsely on the sidelines". MacNeice's poetry voiced the same objections, going so far as to proclaim an Irish disgust with myths of the Irish past: in 'Valediction' (1934) MacNeice felt he had to

Take part in, or renounce, each imposture;
Therefore I resign, good-bye the chequered and the
                                        quiet hills
The gaudily-striped Atlantic, the linen-mills
That swallow the shawled file, the black moor where
                                        half
A turf-stack stands like a ruined cenotaph;
Good-bye your hens running in and out of the white
                                        house
Your absent-minded goats along the road, your black
                                        cows
Your greyhounds and your hunters beautifully bred

Your drums and your dolled-up Virgins and your
                                        ignorant dead.

Against such impostures, Longley pursues more nuanced ways of thinking about Ireland and Irish landscape, not only in MacNeice, but in several lesser-known writers, among them the Ulster poet John Hewitt.

Most of us in this line of work became poetry critics because we wanted to show other folks what we liked, and why. The jobs that most need doing, though, often involve showing what we can't like: clearing out rubbish, cleaning up, putting out fires. Much of this volume does just such negative work, clearing away not only ideas Longley hates but writers she dislikes. Declan Kiberd, Ted Hughes, and (less convincingly) Heaney come under fire for "Celticist" or "ethno-critical" tendencies. Another juicy target is Eavan Boland, whose "reception in America… combines the critical permissiveness licensed by literary Irishness with the permissiveness licensed by literary feminism". And then there is Tom Paulin, whom Longley more or less covers in boiling oil: in his Hazlitt book, in his writings on poets, and in his political pronouncements, Paulin's "utopian conceits simplify the relation between language and politics"; "his criticism depends on poetic license" in ways no critic should.

Though her attack pieces can be lots of fun, Longley's most durable insights arrive when she is least the critic of critics, and most the literary historian. A superb essay on Larkin examines his debts to Cyril Connolly, his early dependence on "decadence", his imputed "narcissism" and his "philistine mask". An intriguing piece on the early careers of Heaney, Michael Longley and Derek Mahon examines their debts to American New Criticism and the poets it favored – Wallace Stevens, Richard Wilbur, Hart Crane; another essay circles historiographical questions before investigating poets' responses to the 1994 cease-fires. My favourite aspect of the volume is the intelligent sympathy Longley brings in these essays to writers she favours – to Larkin, to Thomas, to Mahon, to MacNeice. My least favourite aspect is the prose style, for which Bloodaxe ought to bear some blame. "Yet, with the unarticulated English question on the literary as well as political agenda, morbid symptoms of hegemonic anxiety lurk beneath the pluralistic surface". "Overall, historians (sometimes fighting one another) were drawn into a symptomatic *Kulturkampf* on the volatile Irish interface between historiography and politics". "A subtext [in MacNeice's prose] may be the encounter between a classicist / philosopher and failures to take responsibility for literary-critical language". That is: MacNeice's training with Latin and Greek alerted him to sloppy writing. Would we all were so alert.

Though she insists that we judge poems as works of art, Longley is only intermittently interested in how poems sound. Mostly she insists that our senses of the world and of the past ought to come into play in our reading. "Any genuine poem", she goes so far as to say, "in some sense explains its own historical moment to the reader". (The trouble with "most of the socio-political vocabularies inflicted on 'poetry since 1945'", Longley explains, is not that they situ-

ate poetry in history, but that they do so in too-simple ways). Longley praises poems when their intellectual and ethical stances strike her as valuable, or careful, or true. Her prose, her mode of argument by accretion, and her constant attention to current debates, more often suit an academic audience than a broader span of readers: this book will not widen her public. It will, however, give interested readers a series of closely-argued and well-defended positions about Ireland, ecology, poets and poetry, positions from which anyone could learn. MacNeice declares, in an aphorism Longley quotes, "All that a critic can do is lay stepping stones over the river". Here, then, are some big, flat, solid, carefully-placed, and useful stones.

CHRIS GREENHALGH

"Lively isn't an active enough word to encompass the man's range of moods, style, and specific bees-in-bonnet", said the late Bill Turner in these pages. Greenhalgh has a strikingly extravagant Epicurean wit that ought to be more noticed. He is drawn to exotic biology and technology and finding outrageous human parallels. In 'A Short History of Milk' he develops the conceit of his wife filling the bath with warm milk to bathe *à la* Cleopatra. But the milk starts to set and she has to be dug out. It is an exercise in lactatory erotics carried off with panache. In 'The Glass Blower' the frailty of blown glass bubbles becomes a metaphor for a miscarriage: "I imagine for a moment / all the flasks / breaking through their wall, / floating free and letting fall / a host of glaucous bubbles". He also has a macabre streak. The title poem of his second collection *Love, Death and the Sea Squirt* (Bloodaxe, 2000) refers to that creature's habit of devouring its own brain after copulation. In 'An Encounter', the protagonist tries to take advantage of a woman in a train as it enters a tunnel, only to find that she doesn't resist because she is dead.

THE UNDERSEA WORLD OF JACQUES COUSTEAU

While my mother choked on a fish-bone,
I was shuffled into another room

to watch *The Undersea World of Jacques Cousteau.*
Clouds of bubbles slid giddily from

a diver's mouthpiece
while my mother coughed up blood.

Outside, a seethe of snowflakes placed
feathery rims on the leafless trees.

The ocean teemed with presences.
My mother's face took on

a distressing error in form.
The ocean generated a sad music all its own.

Ambulance lights dyed the snow blue.
The crew gathered for one last tableau.

THE INVENTION OF ZERO

Nature adores a vacuum –
a few bits of light
snagged on nothingness.

The Romans understood the plenum
but it was the Arabs
who invented zero,
summoning nothing *ex nihilo*.

Descending into Heathrow,
sclerotic arteries of traffic glow
like a dye injected into the blood.

Office windows flash their patterns –
lit and blank, like the ones and zeros
of binary code.
The river is a broad gap of darkness.

Above – the moon like an entry-wound,
white beyond bleaching,
the end of abstraction;
a perfect blank.

And back home,
on the answerphone
a rubbed spot on the surface
of the silence

where voices have been erased.

PAULINE STAINER

Pauline Stainer is a poet of intense epiphanies, working images from science and fine art into her highly chiselled poems. She often writes about visual artists such as Cecil Collins, Alfred Wallis, Puvis de Chavannes. After New Generation she moved to the Orkneys, a place highly congruent with pared down elemental imagery: "How it glitters – the land / between ebb and incoming // arctic terns fencing with mirrors / between the islands // the drowned pressing spindrift / to their faces / like little veronicas". Her latest collection, *Parable Island* (Bloodaxe, 1999), has many poems from this period. She has now returned to Essex. Her imagery can be extremely gorgeous: "...fire-flies / through green solar spectacles, young lobsters, hauled up dripping, / their claws lapis lazuli / against the light".

THE HANGAR GHOSTS

They come
as the hare dozes
in the dustless air

desultory
in their flying helmets
between huge drums of straw

silent, allspeaking
against the bruiseless blue,
as if the fuselage

still judders through
their bone-marrow
between sorties

and the sky,
serious with snow,
closes behind them.

LANDFALL

after Cavafy

We have seen everything –
clouded leopards,
speckled ox and delicate owl,
revolution
in imperial orchards

the oil-slick of ships
lying in quarantine
under the volcano,
the bright green bones
of the garfish

water silkworms,
that last stitch
in a sailor's shroud
through gristle
between the nostrils

turquoise from Sinai,
vermilion, turmeric,
indigo-merchants
in their summer kiosks,
the grafting of the golden peach.

We travelled lighter
than the purple heron
leaving its footprint
on the steps
of the Buddha.

How can we keep
the beautiful error
of never having arrived,
when winds blow
through the gantries

from the Great Divide?

JANE HOLLAND

Island Photographic

Jane Holland's route into poetry was the unusual one of snooker, in which she was briefly a professional until she was expelled from the game for supposedly bringing it into disrepute. Snooker is actually a good metaphor for poetry: angling off the cush is like setting up a rhyme scheme, full rhymes give off a satisfying clack; as Lawrence Sail memorably writes in 'Snooker Players', snooker is "The rounded image of reason. One click and cosmology thrives". In 'Baize Queens' she writes; This is not life // but it's as near dammit / when the green's running smooth / as silk and you're thirty points ahead". Besides snooker, she writes well of the eternal verities: 'The Newel Post' is a pivot around which life turns: "I recognise her by her changing thread. / I am that point along the passageway / where flesh and spirit tremble into wood". Her one collection to date is *The Brief History of a Disreputable Woman* (Bloodaxe, 1997).

LOVE SONG FOR A GARGOYLE

Speak, rain-stone,
prodigal son of the buttress,

springing like a fist
foot-first from the mother,

foothold of birds
and deluge-summoner.

Tip your black throat back
into the pitch and swell

of stone breasts, loose
the bright tide dowsing her thighs.

Not master nor mastered,
mouth-piece of frogs: sing, speak, croak

the song of the disinherited,
the loveless, the bastard.

Teach me the purity
of decadence, how it strips flesh

to a shipwreck. Place
rough hoof and tongue on it.

Up here, wind takes toll,
buffets the sky

against the bluster of stunned ground,
stone-shod and blind.

You crouch above stirred air,
stiff impetus.

Drumming your wind-heels high
over rain and river

you dance for love, drenching
the silt with shudder.

A knucklebone ladder, a cage
of faith, have climbed

to leap out from this peak,
your singing spine.

AT THE LIGHTHOUSE

Its cold steel eye swung
to dust our heads
below the scruffy creak of pines,
bald old men staring
at the black line
of the Mediterranean.
There was always dust there;
dust in our lungs
and in rope sandals.
We climbed the tilting path
to the lighthouse,
glanced in through the porthole
of the chapel.
From the viewing platform
at two francs a time
the bay was no longer
a silver fish
landed on its side.
You moved off into the dark,
the glowing target

of your cigarette
something to lock onto,
burning the retina.
I should have kept you
shadowy, elusive
as those fairy lights heaving
a half-moon bay.
But we had only months
before we fell apart,
swivelling the lens
to face our hinterland,
each trap at last
revealing what it was,
thick swimming dust
fused in the glare
of that cold steel eye.

JOHN STAMMERS

John Stammers has reinvented the flâneur for our times. His dandified wit is refreshing coming from someone as earthy and grounded in working class life as he is. His models are American: in an interview with Hugo Williams he has said: "Confessional in-your-face sexual rhymester Sexton and urban conversational aesthete O'Hara. Put those two together and you won't be a million miles away from what I'm doing". Outrageousness is something the English rarely carry off but Stammers looks like making a go of it. His narratives are packed with sharp designer detail and the relish for exotic language conveyed in a way that never alienates the reader. Perhaps this is his secret: he makes the reader feel complicit in his world even if actually they are poles apart. *Panoramic Lounge-bar* (Picador, 2001), reviewed on p.79, is the most achieved and entertaining debut for some years.

THE INFANTA OF CASTILE RIDES OUT WITH LEOPARD, PARROT AND MANDOLIN

On the back of her great pachyderm, accompanied by acolytes,
the child-princess of the extended Castilian hegemony
waves at peons and sucks orange segments dusted

                        with castor sugar.

Her elephant passes through the eye of the castle's portal,
nods languorously, his trunk,
made of rubber to the modern eye,
creases as he raises the prehensile nostril
to deal with a bluebottle
that has shone its blue-green carapace
across the face of the Cid and his horse's bronze mane.
The nose despatches
two hundred and fifty million years of evolving.
The white leopard regards the parrot;
the parrot clacks its beak with a clacking sound.

The Infanta encourages the mandolin player with a pig:
"Play up, play up, Emilio, today is a day for song!"
"As all days!", responds the *mandolinero*.
The *leopardo blanco*, in its snow-line raiment,
handles the heat with mere *nobleza*;
its tail undulates like the mountain roads above the city.
Our *princesa* hums her most favourite ballade,
sublime and orangey, with her orange dyed lips,
child godling of the orange city –
the thrum of the mandolin, the clack of the parrot
as it sees itself seen in the eye of the leopard.

¿QUE PASA?

There is a little of everything in everything
Anaxagoras

Lavish rays of the flagrant sun cascade on the esplanade
or coruscate the way H_2SO_4 does, spilt on a lab floor.
A grey (or ash) acacia sweeps a sombrero from its head
making like a *ranchero* on a talcum-white *caballo*
that clops along in the shower of solar-wind particles
whose slavish job it is to bombard the Earth from space today
Hombre, esta muy bueno aqui, muy, muy bueno.

The terracotta soil of the area merely expresses
the downright red of an Andalusian hemipode,
its feathers drenched in henna,
or a post-nuptial bedsheet doused in chicken blood
that threatens a reprise
of the madness aria from Lucia de Lammermoor –
you know the one where she comes out
with it all spattered down her front
and gets into *Eduardo! Eduardo!* and all that,
Eduardo! Eduardo! and all that.
You would rend the nails from your fingers
with the beauty of it, those exquisite trills
embedded in gothic death.
                              It's that even here,
here in the epicentre of a chilli enchilada,
the ice cubes in the glass hold out against it,
little visitants of the cold realms.

Out-classing the debuts

By Jane Holland

JOHN STAMMERS
Panoramic Lounge-bar

Picador, £6.99
ISBN 0 330 48076 6

JOHN STAMMERS' FIRST collection is peopled with the likes of Frank O'Hara, Gilbert and Sullivan, James Joyce, Roddy Lumsden, and Greta Garbo. A motley enough crew to be found at any watering-hole, but in Stammer's *Panoramic Lounge-bar*, most appear to be taking on new identities, transformed by the act of memory into startling metaphors for the poet's experiences. Others stubbornly resist definition, until resistance itself becomes a metaphor, as in the has-to-be-read-to-be-believed 'Listening to his Record Collection

with Roddy Lumsden', where a tongue-in-cheek Stammers concludes that:

Only the lonely
can know the euphony of Roddy.

I'm laughing here, but it's only with appreciation for Stammers' unpredictable and throwaway humour. His talent as a poet is real and unmistakeable. And like one of his heroes, the American poet Frank O'Hara, there is a sense in these poems that sleight-of-hand – jokes, anecdotes, popular references, pastiche – is being used to divert us from the guiding intelligence behind the juggler behind the poet. Blessed with a light touch, Stammers seems to lack that bitter political edge which burdens so much postmodernism with unnecessary self-consciousness.

One of Stammers' great strengths is an ability to leap from one sort of poem to another without hesitation, putting on different voices from his large cast of internal characters. His chosen forms in this collection are varied and highly intriguing, their slick half-rhymes and occasional off-beat line endings resulting in a poetry which demands continual attention as well as applause. For in the tradition of great mythic poetry, Stammers is an instinctive shape-changer, and one who enjoys surprising the reader with playful and unexpected imagery:

> If I were a reticulate snake, perhaps, I would lick
> our odour from the air above the bed...

If I had to produce one gripe about *Panoramic Lounge-bar*, it would probably be the fact that too many poems in this collection, like people meeting each other for the first time, seem to need an introduction before they can be fully appreciated by the reader. I was often left wondering what the story was behind a poem, or who exactly was being addressed, as in poems like 'Nom de plume', 'On Your Last Evening Together', 'Certain Sundry Matters', or even the utterly superb 'Testimony'. The latter has to be the finest poem in the collection, electrifying in its closely-described detail. It deserves lengthy quotation, especially the second stanza where the poet stopped at the General Post Office in Dublin and

> inserted an interpretative finger into bullet
> holes typed there on the wall in belt-fed lines:
> the beautiful stone, the terrible queerness
> of just standing there with the paths the bullets had
> taken
> passing right through me.

But even in this poem I want more a clear-cut explanation of the poem's origins. For instance, who is the poet's Virgil-like companion through the streets of Dublin, and is it Yeats at the end whose *Collected Poems* are finally located in the bookshop:

> unread and silent, straight from his tongue,
> which I held out to you and you took hold of
> so it spanned our two hands like an arc of electric
> that cracked and spat between us –
> both wanting to let go, each unable to.

Perhaps such questions are irrelevant beside the poetry itself. Yet the poem almost seems to invite them from the reader, with its intriguing air of both mystery and intimacy.

While I loved such indications of future strength from Stammers, my favourite poems here were of the more playful kind. The humour in *Panoramic Lounge-bar* is hugely infectious. From the beginning, I found myself wondering if John Stammers fancies himself as a Noel Cowardlike figure, whim-

sical and dry as he leans against some imaginary piano in his silk dressing-gown. This persona is perfectly illustrated by his hilarious opening poem, 'Nom de plume', with its arbitrarily-named flowers and its air of brittle 'twenties sophistication: "How beautiful the Anstruthers are, despite everything". But by the end of the collection, as in 'The Tell' for instance, his humour seems to have veered off in a somewhat darker direction, though stunning lines like –

> We, down High Holborn, and full up with libretto,
> home after the Mikado, loped

– from 'Torch', demonstrate that the tongue-in-cheek element of *Panoramic Lounge-bar* is never far from the surface.

But as a postmodern love-poet, John Stammers could certainly give Roddy Lumsden a run for his money. In the beautifully lyrical 'Spine', I even sensed a sidelong glance at Lumsden's 'Tricks for the Barmaid', the poet here attempting to seduce a bookshop assistant, all "hip and leg and serendipitous slink", with his choice of titles:

> I ask for
> A Scandinavian Book of Love Poems.
> I need to show her, you see, that Love
> is also a form of esoteric lament from Norway
> held in the hand of a stranger.

But I would not say that Stammers is at his best when writing of love. In 'Breakages', Stammers compares his lover's laugh to one by Garbo (though, in true postmodern fashion, the cited "short film of Garbo" only exists in his imagination) where

> she throws her shoulders into laughter, the sky goes
> dark
> and all the glasses on the drinks table go to pieces.

While this is a lovely and neatly-executed love poem, I felt that the second stanza here should have been written in the past tense for maximum impact.

But this is only a debut collection and such gripes are possibly unfair. Indeed, the fact that I found it so hard to remember that *Panoramic Lounge-bar* is a first collection stands witness to John Stammers' sheer talent and technical expertise, outclassing other debuts around it with the ease and confidence of a born poet.

PETER REDGROVE

Justin Slee

Adjust your maps, Falmouth is Cookham. Peter Redgrove's alchemical art is something like Stanley Spencer's, minus the religion. Throughout his career Peter Redgrove has been a one-man orchestra, harmonizing themes that most people hear only dimly, if at all. It is hard to talk of themes in the conventional sense because each poem contains so many touchstones that reverberate through all the poems; an electrical web of being connects human beings to the physical universe in his work. Redgrove's characteristic subjects include water, spiders, the spoors left by all creatures, including humans, orchards, wasps, cider, menstruation, infrastructure (as in the poems here). His characteristic form in recent years has been the tripartite staggered line, reminiscent of Lawrence Ferlinghetti. This line doesn't figure at all in the *Selected Poems* published in 1999.

AT THE OLD POWERHOUSE

(Kingston on Thames)

A swan stretching
            its neck like a javelin speeds
                        a couple of metres
Above the roughened river,
            the stridor of its breath-shaped
                        wings like the creaking
Of a supple switch, a whipstock;
            descending further, the swan steps
                        across the water in five
Giant strides, in five
            mighty braking steps, settles
                        its own foldings
Among the waterfoldings, tucks
            its wings into its armpits, shrugging
                        them in, and yachts onward
As a serenely-sailing ornamental waterbird
            reborn out of the turbulent and draughty
                        air-voyager;
The river glitters like errant electricity
            and a watermusic floats downstream,
                        a jazz funeral no less
With a band and a catafalque and a small black barge
            full of golden instruments;
                        the powerhouse draws itself up

To attention like the old soldier
　　　　　　　it is; I expect smoke from the broken
　　　　　　　　　　　　chimneys, from the colossal
Hearth-chambers, but those
　　　　　　are swifts coiling on the air
　　　　　　　　　　as the music coils
In the air that rushes
　　　　　sonorously through
　　　　　　　　the river-doubled
Trumpets and trombones.

PENELOPE SHUTTLE

Jane Brown

Eavan Boland said of Penelope Shuttle's poetry: "The voyages of child-birth, of love, of growth widen out the lyrics and seek their arrivals in emblems and symbols that have the power of truth". Shuttle writes animistic poetry, and is not afraid of the Pathetic Fallacy ("a little fear-ful river") or exclamation: "O Dew frost", "O blossom tree", or of gorgeousness, as in 'Geologies' which features pages of precious stones and minerals: "Cornflower blue / of the sapphires / of Kashmir / Peridot greens / like the leaves of waterlilies…" Her poetry is concerned with the moods of people and of nature, especially rain, clouds, wind, the sea. She writes often and well of bed, whether for sleep and dreams or sex: "When we meet and join we hold our breaths / then breathe out all the burning novelty of our bodies, / a big vapour furling into the room, flag / made from our clear-sky flesh, our unearthly diplomacy". Her latest collection is *A Leaf out of his Book* (Oxford Poets / Carcanet, 1999).

from ECLIPSE X 4

"For the eclipse happens at times when the light is defective."

TAKEOVER

The sky takes over,
the moon takes over

The moon and her shadow take over,
so does the earth,
all poised in their line dance

Their skills, survivals and synchronicities
take over,

this is their version of life minus the sun,

silent, dimmed, charmed, brief,
a change for the worse

Look away now

The sun rolls back into place,
vast solar suttee blazing again
Two minutes and fifty seconds? Nice try, moon

* * *

Eclipse eclipsed by cloud,
by rain

Eclipse rage?

Think of Basho,
visiting the Kashima Shrine
for the famed rising of the full moon
and being frustrated by the rain

"such a long way to come only
to look at the dark shadow of the moon"

As if moons and eclipses
chose to be hidden, veiled, absent,

too good for the likes of us,
even Basho,
scribe to the world,

even he not admitted to marvels

* * *

THE BAT OF TOTALITY

(for Jane Tozer)

Sombre eclipse, more Scriabin than Chopin
Tenebrous eclipse, more Bruckner than Ravel

A drag of silver over the sea's sky:
rain or moon shadow?

No one can tell –
yet when the brakes of the cosmic car tighten

to a standstill
we feel this unseen eclipse in our bones,

brains, hearts, genes,
as evident as if we saw it through solar filters

Eclipse more inner than outer

until the swoop of total dark –
longest two minutes of my life,

including any two minutes
of the hours I was in labour.

Near Helston, a lone bat woke,
skidaddled across a friend's field,

maybe thinking,
where are my mothers, my fathers and my brothers,
my sons and my daughters,

my kin, my matrikin,
all my affines?

Delight is the Emotion

by Sophie Hannah

WENDY COPE

If I Don't Know

Faber, £7.99
ISBN 0571 209 556

RARELY CAN A new poetry book be accurately described as "eagerly awaited", but Wendy Cope's new collection certainly is. Her two previous collections, *Making Cocoa for Kingsley Amis* and *Serious Concerns*, were both best-sellers, and *If I Don't Know* deserves to be one too. Cope's fans will find plenty of the sort of witty, rhyming poems about men, relationships and the literary life for which she is well-known, but anyone who is waiting to cry, "Light verse!" will find it hard to make this accusation stick; for every witty rhyming poem in this book, there is a quieter, more elegiac and philosophical one:

> Months ago I dreamed of a tulip garden,
> Planted, waited, watched for their first appearance,
> Saw them bud, saw greenness give way to colours,
> Just as I'd planned them.
>
> Every day I wonder how long they'll be here.
> Sad and fearing sadness as I admire them,
> Knowing I must lose them, I almost wish them
> Gone by tomorrow.
>
> ('Tulips')

Whereas *Serious Concerns* dealt with the misery of being single and looking for love, the main theme of *If I Don't Know* is how difficult it is to be happy when you know that happiness must end. Poem after poem is a celebration of life balanced by an awareness of its transience:

> The book I've been reading

> rests on my knee. You sleep.
> It's beautiful out there –
> fields, little lakes and winter trees
> in February sunlight,
> every car park a shining mosaic.
>
> Long, radiant minutes,
> your hand in my hand,
> still warm, still warm.
>
> ('On a Train')

There is a simplicity, a descriptive minimalism, about Cope's poetry that is extremely effective; in 'Idyll' she gives us only a few concrete details, yet manages at the same time to make the whole scene spring to life:

> ...We won't talk all the time. I'll sit back
> Contemplating shadows on the red-brick path.
>
> And marvel at the way it all turned out.
> That yellow begonia. Our gabled house.
>
> Asked to imagine heaven, I see us there,
> The way we have been, the way we sometimes are.

A less talented poet would have described the red-brick path for four lines, the begonia for another four, and the house for five or six, burying all three under piles of words until they were hardly visible. Cope doesn't need to. When, in 'If I Don't Know', the title poem, she writes, "I sit on the swing and cry", such is her creative authority that, without a single physical detail, the swing becomes not merely a swing, but the swing, and we can picture it clearly. This is so refreshing in the current poetic climate, with so many alleged poets overdoing the physical description because they are desperate to give their work some poetic flavour, like bad cooks who put too much sherry in a trifle just to make it taste of something – anything.

Though Jason Strugnell does not feature in this book, Cope is still very funny on the subject of poets and poetry readings:

> Everybody in this room is bored.
> The poems drag, the voice and gestures irk.
> He can't be interrupted or ignored.
>
> Poor fools, we came here of our own accord
> And some of us have paid to hear this jerk.
> Everybody in the room is bored.

The silent cry goes up, "How long, O Lord?"
But nobody will scream or go beserk
He won't be interrupted or ignored

Or hit by eggs, or savaged by a horde
Of desperate people maddened by his work.
Everybody in the room is bored

Except the poet...

('A Reading')

Cope, unlike the poet in 'A Reading', can get away with calling one of the poems in this collection 'Being Boring', which is a conceit that works well because the poem contradicts its title so comprehensively. It's a moving, funny and satisfying love poem:

There was drama enough in my turbulent past:
Tears and passion – I've used up a tankful.
No news is good news and long may it last.
If nothing much happens, I'm thankful....

Someone to stay home with was all my desire
And, now that I've found a safe mooring,
I've just one ambition in life: I aspire
To go on and on being boring.

Despite the contentment and sense of romantic fulfilment in some of these poems, Cope can still be her acerbically critical old self when commenting on the relationship between the sexes, so those of her fans who are still disillusioned with romance and seeking solace shouldn't lose heart:

He tells her that the earth is flat –
He knows the facts, and that is that.
In altercations fierce and long
She tries her best to prove him wrong.
But he has learned to argue well.
He calls her arguments unsound
And often asks her not to yell.
She cannot win. He stands his ground.

The planet goes on being round.

('He Tells Her')

It is hard to write poems of two, three or four lines that feel substantial and satisfying, but Cope

manages it in this book as she did in her two previous collections. 'Firework Poem II' (which was commissioned, and had to be short enough to fit on a firework) reads, "Write it in fire across the night: /Some men are more or less all right". 'Timekeeping' is hilarious, instantly memorable:

Late home for supper,
He mustn't seem drunk.
"The pob cluck", he begins,
And knows he is sunk.

The range of this outstanding collection is incredible – from translations to the long narrative poem 'A Teacher's Tale' – but the poems all have something in common: they could only have been written by Wendy Cope. Her authorial persona – plain-speaking, serious-minded, contrarily witty – is unlike anyone else's, and the most refreshing thing about her work is that it effortlessly avoids the limp homogeneity that seems to infect so much contemporary poetry. Who but Cope could have written 'A Hampshire Disaster' (inspired by the headline "Shock was the emotion of most" in the Hampshire Chronicle)?

When fire engulfed the headquarters
Of the Royal Winchester Golf Club
In the early hours of Wednesday morning,
Shock was the emotion of most.

But fear had been the emotion
Of some who saw the flames, and admiration
For the courage and skill of the firefighters
Was another emotion felt.

At the loss of so much history –
Cups, trophies and honours boards –
Sadness is now the emotion
Of many Winchester golfers.

Stoical resignation was the emotion
Of the club captain, as he told the *Chronicle*
"The next procedure will be to sort out the insurance.
Life must go on".

Delight is the emotion of this reviewer.

PATIENCE AGBABI

Lyndon Douglas

Kwame Dawes has said of Patience Agbabi: "[she is] constantly willing to experiment not just with forms, but with various moods, various tones, various airs, from the urban funk of the drug-induced madness of 'Ajax' to the staid elegy for a veteran of World War II in 'Poppies and Fresh Ribbons' ". Street credibility vies with street vulnerability in the poems in her second collection, *Transformatrix* (Payback, 2000). There is the bravado of 'Ms de Meanour': "The bastard child / of Barbara Cartland and Boy / George, in a sequinned shift, checking the time / on a Rolex…" Her rap couplets, as in 'Open Sesame', are witty : "They call me Jax, though my real name's Eva / the whole of the Jackson Five rolled into one serious diva".

SKINS

It's not like you don't turn me on.
Every time you walked past
I thought "She's fit".
Come-to-bed eyes.
We both want to
feel my skin

against your skin.
It's not like you're on
or I'm changing into
a woman. It's my past.
Look into my eyes.
I just wanted to fit

in. A misfit.
Mixed-race but light-skinned,
brown hair, blue eyes,
bootboy with a hard-on.
I passed.
I had to.

Then I got this tattoo.
I did it in a fit
of rage. It soon passed.

You want to read my skin?
Whatever turns you on.
I closed my eyes

and put my soul on ice,
denied a Black dad, too
terrified to let on.
I wore the outfit,
marched with the skins.
I don't like to talk about the past,

I hate my past.
My big lie reflected in their eyes,
their hatred in my skin.
With this tattoo
I'm a walking Photofit.
That's why I keep my clothes on.

It's past midnight. I'll call a cab if you want me to.
But your eyes know how to fit
a condom like a second skin. Come on . . .

STEP

into my shoes, Imelda, said the dead queen
so I placed my right foot in her glass coffin,
glimpsed a black and white and ruby premonition
of her daughter, rigid with my Cox's poison.

The queen and I were lovers. We told no-one.
She died in childbed. Every day I'm broken
to see her killer mocking my reflection.
The mirror never lies. Neither does passion.

I'm granite cold during my confession.
They call me witch, harlot, slave to fashion
and sentence me to dance in wrought iron
shoes hell-hot from the oven. So I step

into my deathbed, lined with scarlet satin,
studded with broken glass, next to my queen.

JOHN WHITWORTH

John Whitworth is an almost exact contemporary of Wendy Cope, Kit Wright and Peter Reading, poets who matter to him. He is one of the light verse school and his early narrative poems have a bounce and brio and a feel for contemporary suburban life rare in modern poetry. He can make light verse tell as well, as in 'Careless Love' which weaves a tale of adultery through the Homebase world of suburban barbecue lots. For many years he wrote topical verse for the *Independent*, and *Poetry Review*'s Sonnet History series of portraits, published in *From the Sonnet History of Modern Poetry* (Peterloo, 1999). *Landscape with Small Humans* (Peterloo, 1993) often strikes a Betjemanesque note in its evocations of a 1950s Metroland childhood: "My father's hurrying to the Board of Trade, / Down New Elizabethan colonnades. / Sycamores weep their still-imperial map / Of leaves and fat Churchillian conkers drop". His new book, *The Whitworth Gun*, is due from Peterloo this autumn.

TWO CLASSY SONNETS

i.

I am proud of my working class roots.
I will root for my working class pride.
By the soles of my working class boots,
By the hair of my working class hide,
By the pint in my working class glass,
By the crack in my working class arse,
By the working class heart on my sleeve,
By the working class soul that's inside,
By the working class puke on the floor,
Let me roar with my working class crowd,
I BELIEVE! I BELIEVE! I BELIEVE!
I am proud to be loud (it's allowed),
Let me crow with my working class roar,
I AM PROUD! I AM PROUD! I AM PROUD!

ii.

By the hairs on my working class chest,
By the sweat on my working class brow,
By the crack in my working-class arse,
By the holes in my working class vest,
You're a middle class snake in the grass,
You're a middle class son of a bitch,
And your wife is a middle class cow,
By the scratch of my working class itch,
You are leafy suburbanite trash,
You have shat on your birthright for cash,
And may this be my working class vow,
Yes, my working class vow as of now,
That my heart stay as red as a rose is,
Though it gets up your middle class noses.

GRETA STODDART

Greta Stoddart has waited to publish a first collection after having won several prizes over the last few years, including 2nd Prize in the 1998 *TLS*/Blackwells Competition. She was shortlisted for the Geoffrey Dearmer Prize last year, and her work has appeared in many magazines, including the *TLS*, the *Independent on Sunday* and *Verse*, and in the Poetry School anthology *Tying the Song* (Enitharmon, 2000). In her introduction to this selection she says that she aspires "to something beyond the twanging of heartstrings". Her poetry is impressive for its control of formal stanzas and is emotionally direct and moving; her narratives have a curious flavour, as if they're coming from very far off. In 'A Hundred Sheep in a Green Field' she recounts coming on an accident as a child; she describes the scene, then: "I saw beyond this / to a hundred sheep in a green field / eating their cheerless way through the earth". Her collection, *At Home in the Dark*, will be published by Anvil in September.

ERRAND

See that postbox on the hill? It strikes an almost
tragic pose up there where the four roads meet.
In wind and driving rain, in snow and blistered heat
it stands alone like an old messenger, cursed, struck;
dumb and trusted treasurer of this town's tendered notes,
its severances and dried tears, its good luck.

Dusk. A thin rain. A child with a letter skips
slowly to the box, reaches up, then hesitates
– so a simple act, freeze-framed, hinges at fate –
eyeing her mother's shakey hand, the indifferent Queen,
about to slide forever into the black lip.
The lamps stutter on, the street is lit like a scene.

She is not to know what lay in her hands, what power,
if any, she had before she heard the paper's soft
thud that filled her with a sudden sense of loss
as she turned for home, not knowing the reason why,
leaving the letter to its few innocent hours,
nestled among the others, unpilfered, warm and dry.

CONVALESCENCE

I've come from a world where there is no taste,
where nothing happens in a small back room
but a chair sitting still and self-possessed.
For days I watched the cold eternal core
of things, heard the pitiful ring of the phone
(only the mirror did what it always does,
showing me a face I don't, will never, know);
and from the radio came voices of people
who live in a place where things matter.

Slowly though, as embers when blown
can reawake, words have come to their senses
and so to my death and how I've seen it
become a close, uncomplicated thing.
But now, moving into the sun I want
never not to feel that warm hand
through the kitchen window, nor taste
this fierce fruit needling my jaw,
nor see that bird clutch in its beak that straw.

SHEENAGH PUGH

Sheenagh Pugh's reputation as a trenchant critic may have obscured her poetry to some extent but the same quality of fierce independence shines through both. She writes on many subjects and is good at seeing contemporary phenomena in the longer glass of historical context – her poem 'Headsound', about the Walkman for instance. Or the sardonic 'Bumblebees and the Scientific Method', about the supposed impossibility of insect flight (until 1996 when scientists suddenly twigged what the mechanism might be). Like Jenny Joseph with 'Warning', Sheenagh Pugh claims to be fed up with her much anthologized poem 'Sometimes' but poems like that have a life of their own and no longer need the author's protection. She has recently been engaged in a series of poems set in the world of fan fiction: these have appeared on her website (www.geocities.com/sheenaghpugh/) and will also appear in her next collection, *The Beautiful Lie*, due from Seren in the Autumn.

KENSITAS FLOWERS

Each card opens to show a flower
embroidered on a square of silk,

and a brief history. "There's education
in them cigarette cards", she used to say

throatily. She'd ease one, between thin
yellow fingers, out of a new packet

and pass it over. I'd stroke the threads
of moss rose, gentian, sweet-sultan

and read their folklore. *Romans scented
their baths with lavender.* At Christmas

we'd give her lavender bathcubes,
but they never masked the stale smoke.

I still read her cards, now and then,
getting an education. Scabious

is the widow's flower, nasturtiums glow
phosphorescent at night, cornflowers

can blunt a sickle. Here's a pretty one:
its white stars stand for contentment.

Nicotiana, widely held sacred
and credited with great healing powers.

MALT

From the west, past the wide freight sidings
and the great stadium glassing the sky
so insolently.

From the north, down the valley lines
that leached coal and iron, and then the people
who had nothing left.

From the east, running by a long road
all DIY and flatpacks, down to the malls,
the cafe bars, the theme pubs.

Whichever way, you walk out
of Central Station into that smell,
a sweet wall of malt

from the brewery. I've known folk be sick.
Me, I don't notice any more,
or I've come to like

something about it. How do you end up
cherishing a skyline, a face,
not for any beauty

or singleness, but because you know them?
I never stayed anywhere long enough
for the cataracts

of familiarity to cloud my eyes.
The best station was always the one
I hadn't stopped at yet;

a place only had to be new
to make me want to go there.
They say habit

and custom come with age: I think
they make it happen. The tower of St John's
and the long finger

of the Pearl Building probe too far.
I hear myself call this place
not by its name,

but *home*. Time to move. Roots
taste of earth. New skylines. Pain
means you're still alive.

DAVID CONSTANTINE

David Constantine is unusual amongst contemporary poets in applying
a modern, seared diction to reworkings of biblical and classical stories.
His subject matter is sometimes more contemporary, as in 'Bombscare',
about to appear in the Forward of Forwards anthology but whatever the
setting of the poems Constantine's treatment always has a clarity and
moral vigour , without ever being preachy. Sean O'Brien has said of his
poetry: "The mood is both tender and desperate, with something of the
uncanny in its blend of the recognisably human and the apparently
other". All his poetry is sacramental, even when the setting is quotidian.
'Musicians on the Underground' are "...as free as swallows and they
know / what the ghosts felt once and they warn us while we can". In
many of his poems he is waiting for something to happen, as in the
famous title poem of his 1983 collection *Watching for Dolphins*. His
latest collection is *The Pelt of Wasps* (Bloodaxe, 1984).

DOMINION

Dear God, if you can imagine us, Man,
Without a chain-saw in our hands or the gun
Or looking away from the prices on the screen
For half a minute, even then in that
Even by you perhaps unimaginable state

The truth is we're not good enough, never were,
Never will be, we're not fit, we don't fit in,
Nothing will live with us except the viruses
And dogs and lice, nothing likes us down here,
Everything else is subtler, finer, fitter than us.

Take a coral reef: we come visiting
It gives up the ghost, it's a bone-yard by morning,
Spectral groves. And that's us all over,
The ashes, the fall-out, whatever we come near
Even in white, with a gauze over the gob,

We're the kiss of death. Dear God, that day
In Eden when you made Adam boss
What a catastrophe, even you must see it by now,
Anything would have been better than us,
A dodo, for example, a booby, a diplodocus.

SHOES IN THE CHARITY SHOP

It can't be helped, the way our minds turn
When we see worn shoes in a pile,
It is an evolution of our kind
We shan't grow out of. But this is charity
This widow pairing them along a rack and selecting
The worst for the tip, the better for pricing
And bringing out into the front shop
For the poor still walking
To step into. Noblest
Were those worn shoes of women queuing at the bus-stop
And along the pavement shuffling turn by turn
Nearer the counter and to being served
While above their hands
Gripped by the weight of bags and the worry over every penny
And far above their feet
Killing them in those trodden shoes
Gloriously they were squandering breath on stories
A wealth of natter and tattle
And answering back. Their shoes
Would never have passed from the pile to the front shop
So shaped to them, who never wanted charity,
No feet on earth after theirs would have fitted them.

JULIA COPUS

Julia Copus received an Eric Gregory Award in 1994 and her first book, *The Shuttered Eye* (Bloodaxe, 1995), won a Poetry Book Society Recommendation, and was shortlisted for the Forward Prize for Best First Collection. Since 1997 she has been Writer in Residence for the Borough of Blackburn. Maura Dooley has said, "Julia Copus's poems view some of the most turbulent moments in life through a sharp, clear lens: mature, uncomfortably honest, uncompromising". Some reviewers of *The Shuttered Eye* felt that her influences – especially Plath – were too noticeable but that is par for the course in a first collection. What she is after in many of her poems is the primal force behind the surface, like the painter in 'Botanical Artist' who whilst busy with "the raised lateral veins, the spikelets on the mid- / rib and the ear-like lobes" dreams of pulling a mandrake from the ground: "its scream / flew up like a blood-spurt, staining / the night-air". She received an Arts Council Writer's Award this year.

Tolga Baloglu

LAMB'S ELECTRONIC ANTIBIOTIC

Just as a holy man will turn aside
to pray, reflect, and be still before God,
when Lamb's life went from bad to worse he took
to coming here. He'd pull the roof caul-like
over his head. It seemed to be as good
a place as any for the job, this shed,
this backyard makeshift workshop, calm with books
and instruments: a lamp, a UV box
holding the light inside, chastened and quelled.
Through solitude he came to know the world
of scheming and invention and things born
bewildered in half-light: non-stop till dawn
beneath the spell-like clicking of the clock
he holed away and turned his mind to work.
He kept a stash of 10-year-old Laphroaig
beside him as he went, drafting a slug
into a glass to sip, and teased his dreams
from formless fibres into diagrams
of circuits that would govern a machine
for wiping out diseases of the skin.
Under the stream of ions, if I'm right,

contagions, viruses and pox, he thought,
will shrivel back to nothing, retrograde.
Now did his project gather to a head.
Now anything seemed almost possible –
Even the rifts that form between people
are passable, he thought, *after the rot*
is stopped, scraped back, and as often as not
a bridge can be re-grown across a gap –
and in this way he kept from giving up.
At last he held a fledgling prototype
beneath the glow of the oscilloscope,
a photoplotted maze of paths and gates
like plans for some new town, with parks and streets
and one-way systems fixed on acetate,
a place so real he might inhabit it . . .
Soon after, as he peered out at the dark
(and saw his own pale image peering back),
with pink-gloved hands under the window's hush
he rocked the coated circuit in a dish
until the details swam back into view,
clouds of resist uncoiling, breaking free.
The shed was like a ship's cabin that night,
a submarine that cruised beneath the light
of morning where he dreamed his life restored –
the little upturned dinghy in the yard
purged of its woodlice and afloat again
on clear waters under a cloudless sun.
He saw the weeds that poked up through the gaps
between the flags retreat like periscopes,
the moss clumps loosen from the greying thatch,
and in his mind he scaled the house to watch
moss-capsules sealing round their spores, rhizoids
detaching till the thatch's flaky reeds
sprang back to glossy ovate tubes. He planned
to bring the gardens, everything he owned,
back to the newness of that golden roof;
and then to stand beneath it with his wife,
the dark patches of hurt on both their hearts
dissolved away, betrayals and retorts
erased at last, each by the other's side,
the air between them stable, purified.

VERNON SCANNELL

Alan Benson

Vernon Scannell is an exponent of what might be thought a dying art: sensuously evocative formal verse that tries to render recognisable experiences in memorable language. His standard and productivity have remained extraordinarily even over the years. One of Scannell's most appealing traits is his relish for texture and his understanding of how to render this in verse, as in 'Autumn': "It is a time of year that's to my taste, / Full of spiced rumours, sharp and velutinous flavours". He is a poet of *lachrimae rerum* – literally, in the poem of that title, and in his general practice: "In music or those spectral, yet unblurred / Pictures that may flower inside the head, / However bright, faint shades of loss intrude". His latest collection, *Views and Distances,* was published by Enitharmon in April, 2000.

OLD WOUNDS

Long ago the wounds were healed,
and he forgets that they once bled
and burned and blotted out the light
and sumptuous colours of the world,
and filled his unprotected head
with loud but wordless night.

Now each wound quietly lies below
its dark or silver cicatrice
and does not hurt at all, unless
the weather turns and bleak winds blow
with threats, or their fulfilment, of
unpitying hail and snow.

Then pain, or its pale phantom, haunts
the places where it left its prints;
but other kinds of hurt occur:
a half-forgotten tune or scent
can penetrate, and slyly stir
long dormant shades of her.

As when, two days ago, he saw
her cross the street; and there she stood,
her smile against the sun, half-frown,
a look that he had always loved.
Then she was gone. The wound wept raw,
and words seeped out like blood.

REDOLENCES

Gloucester: O, let me kiss that hand!
Lear: Let me wipe it first; it smells of mortality

King Lear: Act IV, Scene VI

Those childhood whiffs, those pungencies
and fragrances, no longer known
except in memory,
still haunt this summer evening and they bring
related images of place and thing,
black jewels of tar on sun-stunned roads,
the creaking of a garden swing.

The garden darkens, and the scents
of honeysuckle, roses, stock,
persist. Though hidden now
from sensible cognition they remain
mysteriously present in the brain
to tease, then cunningly unlock
those little cells of zest and pain.

Sunlight, the yellow smell of hay
in Folly Lane; then counterpoint
of silage and manure;
outside the inn, the breath of various beers
from open door and windows commandeers
the air with whispers redolent
of grown-up secrets, hungers, fears.

Then other odours, not quite lost
to deft imagination's net
that trawls the populous past
for sweet and yeasty scents of hymns and bells,
and sooty reek of lachrymose farewells
as train-doors slam; though we forget,
with luck, that hand, and how it smells.

GEORGE SZIRTES

Clarissa Upchurch

George Szirtes possesses one of the most fluid verse techniques in English poetry, allied to an intense interest in the matter of Europe, deriving from his Hungarian background. It is this unusual combination that gives his poetry its distinctive feel. His most recent book, *The Budapest File* (Bloodaxe, 2000), collected his poems on Hungarian themes that were scattered among his many collections. He sometimes sounds, with his brisk stanzas and cultural sweep, as Auden might have done had he had roots in Continental Europe: "The ego grinds like a machine. / The voyage out begins in classrooms where / Stout boys in dirty tracksuits clean / ruled sheets of paper to a helpless stare / which pierces the heart..." His book *Metro,* most of which is included in *The Budapest File,* has some very fine evocations of Central European cities: "There are certain places healthy to have lived in: / Certain streets, hard cores of pleasure: / Their doorways are ripe fruit, stay soft and open,/ Exhaling a fragrance of drains and tobacco".

VISITATIONS

As one comes in another goes out. As one
shakes out a tablecloth another is eating
a hearty meal. As one sits down alone
another listens to his lover's heart beating.

As one prays for deliverance, another
delivers a letter or an explosive device.
As one gathers the harvest, his brother
lies in the doorway. As one finds a nice

coincidence between numbers, his neighbour
sees his coins disappear down the waiting slot.
As one man examines the fruit of his labour
his shadow tells beads, counts peas into the pot

or stars in the sky and feels the night wind blowing
on his face with all this coming and going.

*

As one goes out, the other comes in. It is light
in the window where the angel bends
over the stove giving the virgin a fright.
It is bright at the top of the house where the road ends.

There's a distinct touch of gold in the gutter
running with beer. There is translucence
in the chipped saucer with its rim of used butter.
There's a glow on TV. There's a faint sense

of the luminous numinous in the alarm clock
set for six in the morning and a kind of shine
in the mirror the angels have learned to unlock
and enter suddenly and an even harder to define

radiance in the skin, in the shock of dawn
with sheet turned down and bedroom curtains drawn.

Hungary and History

by Hugh Macpherson

GEORGE SZIRTES

The Budapest File

Bloodaxe, £9.95
ISBN 185 224 531X

GEORGE SZIRTES HAS always been an exemplary poet, in all senses. He's written good poetry from the beginning and been recognised for this (Geoffrey Faber Prize, Fellow of Royal Society of Literature etc.); is in many ways very English and yet a refugee from the Hungary of 1956; was encouraged by the poet Martin Bell (1918-78) – a man often seen as providing a link between English

poetry from before and after the war; published by Secker and Warburg, then by OUP, and now has a large new volume from Bloodaxe. Often expected, because of his Hungarian connection, to produce some Audenesque fusion between an English tradition and Europe, he had the good sense to concentrate on his own poetic mythology. Yet he has been extremely interested in his Hungarian roots, visiting in 1984, spending much of 1989 there. Since then he has written many poems about Hungary, and has translated several decidedly interesting books, including a selection of poems by István Vas, novels by Kosztolányi and Krasznahorkai, and, best of all, the stories of Gyula Krúdy's *The Adventures of Sindbad*. (Krúdy's sensibility, one of Hungary's many inspired gifts to Europe, has so far, like all presents too refined for the recipient at the time of handing over, remained ignored among the wrappings.)

Bridge Passages was one of the 1990s titles Szirtes used to indicate his concern to pull together the various influences on his life. That increasingly fruitful playing-off of his English self against his rediscovered Hungarian personality has indeed been one of his strong points for some years, spun together with a third voice created or implied by the meeting of the two others, inspired by and aware of both but encompassed by neither.

The new book *The Budapest File* – with its fashionably of-the-moment title – is an unexpected move in the opposite direction, concentrating on the Hungarian side in isolation. Some of the poems have appeared in previous books, alongside others that had different preoccupations. In his preface Szirtes himself sounds somewhat uneasy about this presentation: "These 'Hungarian' poems appear to look to a phantasmal Budapest as their hub. It feels odd to have them separated from the other poems, a little painful too, like driving an axe down a fault line, but I can see it makes a kind of sense". Earlier he emphasises: "national (let alone nationalistic) concepts are incidental, and often, to my mind, harmful". To the reader who comes to this from earlier collections, it feels like a tidying-up of the normally mutually-reinforcing strands of Szirtes' work.

However, the individual poems themselves are as strong as ever. Commenting on 'Transylvana' – about a visit to a formerly Hungarian part of Romania – he says it is "in many respects a highly photo-journalistic poem" and adds firmly " 'He don't *invent* it', as Peter Reading says of his own reporting" and reinforces the point with "Of course he is right: most poets don't".

History is much in evidence here, but lived history, history that has to be examined to understand yourself and see where you are. We are reminded, forcibly, of how very much the Europe of today is a creation of the horrendous events of sixty years ago. We may say it's all behind us, but the place we've ended up in, where we say that from, has been decided by what happened then.

One of the new poems is called 'The Lost Scouts' and is about Szirtes' attendance at a reunion of his father's pre-war scout group from Budapest. "Being Jewish, most of them died in the war and many went into emigration. After 1989 they began to gather... for a few days every three years". So Szirtes meets the returning

... Mowglis, Sir Galahads,
Chingachcooks, Wolves, all of a mythical
               company...
...

Then came history, and the wolfpacks they cried appeared at the door and demanded their one life and they gave it, like that, and so the evening ends.

> We were saddened to hear of the death of Hugh Macpherson, soon after receiving this review. An appreciation will appear in the next issue.

It's a moving and persuasive poem that has similar force (though a different story to tell) to Louis Malle's film *Au Revoir Les Enfants* about the fate of children in wartime France.

This is poetry which is deeply-felt and intelligent. With poems that are consistently well-crafted, powerful and evocative, *The Budapest File* is a book to get hold of. Szirtes is increasingly revealed as a major English poet – one of those in whom insight and technique combine to focus more and more productively as the years go by.

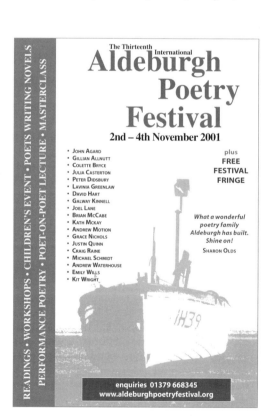

THE REVIEW PAGES

Accept No Substitutes

DAVID WHEATLEY ON THE MAN WHO REALLY IS MULDOON

PAUL MULDOON

Poems 1968–1998

ISBN 0 571 20950 5
Faber, £12.99

WHEN *NEW WEATHER* appeared in 1973 Paul Muldoon was still, just about, a student at Queen's University, Belfast. A technical error led to the entire book being printed in italics, making it look as if his words were straining on the leash, leaning greedily into the future they knew belonged to them. How right they were: within the next decade he had published *Mules, Why Brownlee Left* and *Quoof*, and already it looked as if he had been there forever. Perhaps he has: if Muldoon the student prodigy wasn't bad enough, the timespan announced by *Poems* backdates his *Wunderkind* status another five years. It's enough to make a late starter feel as sour as the lemon which gives this volume its colour: a cross, no doubt, between the lemon sorbet of 'The Frog' and the "lemon stain" left on the poet's flannel sheet in 'Aisling'.

By emulating his fellow Irishman Derek Mahon in publishing a Yellow Book of his own, Muldoon has succumbed to the delicious decadence of publishing a virtual *Collected Poems* before the age of fifty. Mention of Mahon, whose *Collected* appeared in 1999, prompts an irresistible comparison. Some poets revise on these occasions and some poets don't. Mahon doesn't just chop and change but slashes and burns, abolishing stanzas and poems as he goes, and any individual identity his collections may have possessed. Whereas Muldoon simply lines up his eight Faber books and sticks an author's note at the front announcing his certainty that "after a shortish time, the person through whom a poem was written is no more entitled to make revisions than any other reader". It's hard to know whether this means he's reluctant to tinker because he's so splendidly sure of himself or the exact opposite; but then Muldoon's sense of the unitary self has always been given to strange aberrations ("I was standing in for myself, my own stunt double", as he writes in 'Between Takes'). The short answer to Muldoon is probably Yeats on his self-revisions: "They do not know what is at stake / it is myself that I remake". If the original texts emerge from *Poems* unchanged they're probably the only things that do, the one still point around which the world turns and transforms dizzyingly.

Running out of superlatives with which to describe *Quoof*, Michael Hofmann compared it to the founding of a new religion, by which reckoning most contemporary poets are "Muldoonies" of one sort or another, whether devout, lapsed or born again. The religious comparisons don't end there: if *New Weather* to *Quoof* is the Muldoon Old Testament, culminating in entry to the promised land of the US, *Meeting the British* to *Hay* is the New. *New Weather* does a good impersonation of a Garden of Eden, even down to the Fall of Man narrative of its very first poem, 'The Electric Orchard':

> Deciding that their neighbours
> And their neighbours' innocent children ought to be
> stopped
> For their own good, they threw a fence
> Of barbed wire round the electric poles. None could
> describe
> Electrocution, the age of innocence.

In reality it was a *felix culpa*: his innocence is something Muldoon regains and loses over and over again in luminous early lyrics like 'The Sightseers', 'Cuba', 'Anseo', 'Promises, Promises', 'Lunch with Pancho Villa' and 'Gathering Mushrooms', all of them knockout poems, culminating in the great Troubles epic 'The More a Man Has the More a

Man Wants'. That still leaves us with two thirds of *Poems* to go, however, and this is where things start to get complicated.

If there is an awkward or turning-point book in here – Muldoon's John Wesley Harding to use a 'Sleeve Notes'-style analogy – I would nominate not *Madoc* but its predecessor, *Meeting the British*. Anything coming after *Quoof* was going to have a hard time, but what makes *Meeting the British* different is its moving in two new directions simultaneously. There is the hard-edged, almost sarcastic tone of 'Meeting the British', 'Wystan' (from '7, Middagh Street') and 'Bechbretha', the last of which reads like a Tom Paulin poem, as Muldoon has confessed, reminding us of the book's political moment in the wake of the Anglo-Irish Agreement of 1985. And then there is the new "semiotic" Muldoon, visible in effects like the obsessively repeated *rgn* sounds of 'Sushi' (notice how the food begins to go upmarket too from here on), 'Ontario' and 'Chinook' ("their very name / a semantic / quibble").

And then there's *Madoc* itself. Perhaps Muldoon should have emulated Pound's footnote to 'Hugh Selwyn Mauberley' in *Personae* and given the page number where those who'd rather skip ahead can rejoin the book. You're either a believer in *Madoc* or you're not, and if not will probably think it's all downhill from here with the token exception of 'Incantata', the acceptable face of late Muldoon. I for one think you'd be wrong. Confusion, if that's what *Madoc* induces, "is not an ignoble condition", as Brian Friel has said. Critics in search of clues have made much of 'The Briefcase', the short poem dedicated to Seamus Heaney which ends with an eelskin briefcase appearing to metamorphose back into an eel so as to make "for the sea. By which I mean the 'open' sea". Why is the sea closed in quotation marks if it's open? But then, as John Redmond has noticed, "Madoc" itself is a pun on meadóg, the Irish for eel. Slipperiness is all. If surtitled philosophers' names mean nothing to you, just ignore them. Yet even the most outlandish things in the book find ways of connecting with readers' experiences. In theory the entire poem is being scanned from a prisoner's disintegrating eyeball in the futuristic city of Unitel. Teaching the poem in University College Dublin, I was not a little spooked to observe that the campus information screens broadcast a channel also called 'Unitel'. Proof if proof were needed, since the book is full of conspiracy theories, of Muldoon's occult alliance with English Departments around the world.

As for *The Annals of Chile*, my own personal favourite of the eight collections, "Muldoonies" can argue until the cows (Dermot Seymour's 'Cows' of course) come home about the relative merits of 'Incantata' and 'Yarrow', but the other pleasures to be had are no less exquisite. Take the stunning villanelle 'Milkweed and Monarch', for instance, and the climactic point where Muldoon gets the rhyme scheme wrong: "He'd mistaken his mother's name, 'Regan', for 'Anger'", where the pattern dictates that 'Anger' should come before 'Regan'. Getting it wrong registers perfectly the momentary misrecognition of the one for the other as he contemplates his mother's grave.

After the over-arching, all-consuming long poems of the previous two books, *Hay* showed he could still make a collection out of a disparate assembly of short lyrics, with 'The Bangle (Slight Return)' tagged on in the spirit of those *Jaws* posters that read "Just when you thought if was safe to go back in the water...", even if it lacks a bite to match 'Immram' or 'The More a Man Has the More a Man Wants' (though what contemporary long poems don't?). And as for the jokes the book attracted about "middle-aged spread", he might have thought twice about calling one of the shorter poems 'Paunch' if he wanted to avoid that particular jibe.

So what next? Michael Longley has said that the worst introduction he ever got began "Michael Longley is fairly well-known", but for all the years we've spent reading him I'd like to suggest that Muldoon is still extremely well unknown: there's simply no predicting what the next book will be like or about. I've suggested there's a little bit of Muldoon in us all, to the point where he may have begun to blur in our minds with his imitators, but to paraphrase Groucho Marx in *Duck Soup*: this man may read like Muldoon, he may sound like Muldoon, but don't let that fool you: he really is Muldoon, and he really is that good.

"All great artists are their own greatest threat", he wrote of Bob Dylan in 'Sleeve Notes'. It's no back-handed compliment to say that few poets today are bigger threats to themselves than Muldoon. Readers too, fixated on the Muldoon of old, are bound to feel threatened by what he's up to these days. For others the threat is part of the excitement, and books don't come much more exciting than *Poems*. As for the man himself, he looks like he's coping with the strain of it all just fine.

Yesterday's Man

By Ian Sansom

PAUL McCARTNEY

Blackbird Singing: Poems and Lyrics 1965-1999

Faber and Faber, £14.99
ISBN 0 571207 898

ANYONE UNDER THE age of, say, thirty, will probably be blessed with not knowing any Beatles songs, apart from the odd snatches of 'Yesterday', 'Eleanor Rigby' and 'Yellow Submarine' overheard when grandad's been staying and the radio's been retuned from Kiss FM to Radio 2. All the rest is history. *The White Album, Revolver*: they might as well never have been recorded. For the younger reader, therefore, Paul McCartney's *Blackbird Singing* is simply a book of poems by a bloke who used to be in a band. For everyone else, it's perhaps rather more important.

And for no one more so, it seems, than Adrian Mitchell, whose introduction to McCartney's poems and lyrics is an act of homage. "Paul takes risks", writes Mitchell, "again and again, in all of his work". Paul McCartney does a lot of things, but he could hardly be said to take risks: doctors, firemen, mountaineers, Formula One racing drivers, stock-brokers and all the poor people who have to work in nuclear reactors in Russia and Central Asia or in diamond mines in Sierra Leone take risks. If the eminently likeable Mister McCartney were to write a sonnet revealing himself to be a not-very-nice-person then he might be said to be taking risks in his poetry, otherwise, no. "He's not afraid", writes Mitchell, "to take on the art of poetry – which is the art of dancing naked". Were that it were so. If poetry really were the art of dancing naked, then sales of McCartney's book would rival those of Madonna's book *Sex*, or a top-shelf men's magazine. The art of poetry is not the art of dancing naked, unless it's the dance of the seven veils. "There is a real kinship", writes Mitchell, "between Paul's work and poets of today like Brian Patten and Carol Ann Duffy, and also lyric writers like Elvis Costello, Randy Newman and Laurie Anderson". The kinship, presumably, is that they all use words.

But you can hardly blame Mitchell for his enthusiasm, just as you can't blame McCartney for his friends. One should let the poems and lyrics speak for themselves.

> You've got me dancing
> In a figure of eight,
> Don't know if I'm coming or going,
> I'm early or late.
>
> (from 'Figure of Eight')

> But as for me
> I still remember how it was before
> And I am holding back the tears no more,
> I love you.
>
> ('Here Today')

> Maybe I'm amazed at the way you love me all the time
> And maybe I'm afraid of the way I love you,
> Maybe I'm amazed at the way you pulled me out of time,
> You hung me on a line
> Maybe I'm amazed at the way I really need you.
>
> ('Maybe I'm Amazed')

> When I tell you that we'll all be
> Looking for changes
> Changes in the way
> We treat our fellow creatures
> And we will learn how to grow
> When we're looking for changes
> We're looking for changes
> In the way we are
>
> ('Looking for Changes')

Of course, most poetry is no good, whether it's written by Paul McCartney, me, you, or anyone else, and McCartney's poetry is only published by Faber and Faber for the same reason that books get published by the likes of Ann Widdecombe and Edwina Currie. Celebrity sells. And it usually stinks: the novels and poems and paintings and concerts of celebrity-amateurs tend to be over-ripe, under-ripe or simply rotten. Eminence in one field of endeavour does not guarantee excellence in another. Indeed, given the sheer amount of time and effort involved merely in the successful pursuit of a hobby – keeping tropical fish, say – never mind the difficulty of mastering an art form, anything more than competence outside one's own area of expertise seems extremely unlikely. Most people can just about change a fuse, but rewiring is best left to a spark.

Given that McCartney is a songwriter the

chances of his succeeding as a poet actually recede even further. It's a pity, but then the chances of a poet cutting it as a songwriter are even more remote; about as likely in fact as Geoffrey Hill working with Dr Dre and Eminem, or Seamus Heaney going on stage at the Royal Festival Hall in leather trousers. Simon Armitage is only one among many of the younger generation of poets whom one suspects would like to be able to pull it off, but who realises that he can't. In his book *All Points North* he recalls a meeting with a record company executive: "'Of course, I'm sure that writing lyrics will be just the same as writing poetry, only different', says the man. 'Like wanking with the other hand', says you. 'Oh, if it was going to be difficult we wouldn't be asking you to do it', says he, and a minute later you're back out on the New King's Road in the rain, looking for the tube station".

At least Armitage is honest. A song lyric is not a poem, for reasons that hardly need to be stated, except for the benefit of record company executives, academics, and some sensitive teenagers. In his foreword to his own collection of lyrics, Ira Gershwin summarised the difference in a sentence: "Since most of the lyrics in this lodgment were arrived at by fitting words mosaically to music already composed, any resemblance to actual poetry, living or dead, is highly improbable".

A feat improbable, note, but not impossible. In an essay, 'The Thought of Movies', the American philosopher Stanley Cavell explains how Irving Berlin's 'Cheek to Cheek' manages to overcome the odds and pass itself off. Cavell's comments are worth quoting in full, since intelligent comment on song lyrics is about as common as an intelligible lyric by Michael Stipe. "In my early adolescence lines such as:

Heaven, I'm in heaven
And the cares that hung around me through the week
Seem to vanish like a gambler's lucky streak
When we're out together dancing cheek to cheek

– a stanza such as this was what I thought of as poetry – nothing else will be poetry for me that cannot compete with the experience of concentration and lift in such words. It seems to me that I knew this then to be an experience not alone of the behaviour and the intelligence of the words with one another, nor only, in addition, of the wit and beauty of invoking the gambler's run of luck, but that it was an experience of these (though I would

have lacked as yet words of my own in which to say so) together with the drama of using the vanishings of the streak, which is a bad thing, as a simile for the vanishing of cares and the access to heaven, which is a good thing – as if beyond bad and good there were a region of chance and risk within which alone the intimacy emblematized or mythologized in the dancing of Astaire and Rogers is realizable".

There is no doubt that through the process of cultural repetition some of the lyrics included in *Blackbird Singing* have achieved a near mythic status: they have become fully realized. They have become Great Lyrics. Some of the Beatles lyrics are right up there with 'Blowin' in the Wind', 'Waltzing Matilda' and 'My Favourite Things'. Even on paper, phrases such as "Oh I believe in / Yesterday", or "Hey Jude, don't make it bad", or "All the lonely people, where do they all come from", seem possessed of extraordinary power and poignancy. The perceived strength of Great Lyrics is overwhelming: they have proved their power to charm and are impervious to comment or criticism. The memory of the music disarms the critical sense, making it impossible to tackle the words with anything like objectivity. Neither the most strenuous prac. crit. nor an act of post-structuralism could possibly do harm to them. Not even Perry Como could spoil them. You can't even really disagree with the Great Lyrics – Harmony and Melody forever protect them.

Take 'Yesterday'. It's a great song, obviously. McCartney once described it as "the most complete thing I've ever written". But on the page it's clearly lacking in something: the rhymes seem predictable, and the repetitions ponderous. Why? Well, let's put it this way. Back in 1963, the year McCartney famously dreamt the tune for 'Yesterday' in an attic flat in Wimpole Street, Louis MacNeice was rather less famously reviewing Reuben Brower's *The Poetry of Robert Frost* in the pages of the *New Statesman*. "The best lyric after all", wrote MacNeice, "is a lyric plus, but this plusness is the hardest thing for a critic to analyse. Thus with Keats's Odes it is easy to say what the 'Nightingale' has got that the 'Ode to Autumn' has not got but the reverse, which is at least as true, is a far more difficult thing to put one's finger on. What *has* the 'Ode to Autumn' got that the other Odes haven't? Answer: something extremely important". What has the song 'Yesterday' got that Paul McCartney's collected poetry and lyrics hasn't? Answer: something extremely important.

Free the Jack-in-the-box

by John Greening

Anvil New Poets 3
Ed. Roddy Lumsden and Hamish Ironside

Anvil, £9.95
ISBN 0856462837

TEN NEW POETS, of all ages – five women, five men – are here presented to us, together with brief introductions by the the poet Roddy Lumsden and Anvil Press's own Hamish Ironside. Only one – the highly cosmopolitan Indian poet Tabish Khair – has an established reputation (a volume from Penguin India) but several of the writers are likely to be familiar to anyone who keeps up with magazines such as *Acumen* or *Poetry London*. Indeed, both Sarah Wardle and Ros Barber were featured not long ago in *Poetry Review*'s short-list for the Geoffrey Dearmer Award. The arrangement of poets here is alphabetical, so that the winner of that prize, Sarah Wardle, comes as a suitably prestigious finale. Her probing, philosophical work is perhaps a little too literary and self-conscious, her success in using metre and rhyme somewhat erratic – but it's hard to resist 'Word Hill' or her requiem to the BM Reading Room (roll over Stephen Spender!). Apart from those I have mentioned, the book offers selections from Richard Aronowitz, Kathryn Gray, Siân Hughes, A.B.Jackson, Kona MacPhee, Robert Seatter and Julian Turner.

How useful are collections such as this? A dozen poems should be enough to give an idea of a poet's range – but it can also be more bewildering than meeting just one poem in a magazine and really getting to know it, or having the full symphonic experience of a collection. To sit and read through the book fairly rapidly, as a reviewer must, is not the best approach. And in fact it wasn't the breadth that struck me (there is always breadth) so much as the remarkably limited depth of imaginative resources. Surely there is more out there. I kept thinking of Tom and his Midnight Garden: some of these poets have never heard the clock strike thirteen and left their stifling apartments to see what's out there at the back. Yes, there's plenty of sex and city and food and family; but really very little myth and history and spirit and nature.

The poetry our age deserves? It's a Cavalier Age, certainly – something I felt all the more pointedly since I'm currently in the 1600s of Paul Keegan's indispensable *New Penguin Book of English Verse*. There's a Miltonic Puritan in me which cries out for something lost, and which is as it happens, doing very nicely in the New World. Being contemporary doesn't have to involve football and cars and fast-food and the rest of it, as American poets from A. R. Ammons to James Merrill have reminded us. I emerged from this (in many ways impressive) anthology wishing for a little less parochialism, a lot more ambition and universality. It's time the jack-in-the-box climbed out and left the kids' bedroom.

On the other hand, metrically speaking, we have everything America should envy. No need for any New Formalist movement here: the hands (and feet) of Louis MacNeice, John Betjeman, Kit Wright, Wendy Cope are very much present. Most of Anvil's writers are willing to take Dana Gioia's advice and recognise that "no technique precludes poetic achievement".

Of the poets showcased, I was particularly struck by Julian Turner's capacity to mythologise the suburban, while keeping the pentameter fresh and flexible. His wittily mock-heroic golfing poem, 'Penalty of Stroke and Distance' is likely to be a popular anthology piece:

> These are the ones whose rules, exact and pure,
> remind you poor conditions are no excuse,
> who in all weathers will turn out and draw
> their pitching irons cold from rusted pools...

And I also liked his study from a dentist's chair and the nightmare vision of 'Reportage'.

Kathryn Gray's work attracted me, too. It circles around a dense, troubling note, heard in the very first poem, 'Aim', which builds from a youthful memory ("Your brother would bear down the barrel / of a shotgun intent on blasting our summers...") to: "How he fell at a single report, was found / one noon by children – how could we have known / that in there, breathing, under those long days, / he'd met himself coming the other way". This sinister quality returns powerfully in 'Driver' and 'Alibi'; but there is also a playful side to her in 'The Book of Numbers'.

Several of the poets use the idea of play – love-play, sport, childhood – in appropriately formal structures (recollecting Frost's net, perhaps) whether it be Turner's 'Tennis Ball', Ros Barber's 'The Dancer', Siân Hughes' 'The Double' or Robert Seatter's 'Learning Happiness' . Seatter's poems do not seem quite fully achieved, too slack in their rhythms – or perhaps it's just by contrast with the formal work surrounding them. His 'At Central Station, Milan' suggests a possible future direction, however. Hughes, too, has a light touch that sometimes doesn't quite convince. Her 'Secret Lives', which won the *TLS* competition, catches what she does best – and unconsciously describes her own poetic style at the same time:

> Sometimes your dressing gown unhooks
> And slides out under the garden door,
> With three aces up his sleeve...

Ros Barber's is altogether tauter work – narratives of anxiety, uncertainty and defiance – her experience as a teacher of creative writing occasionally evident in the forms, her endings not always well-judged, but often movingly elegiac, as in 'Well' and 'Old School Friends'. The latter poem describes the sudden arrival of well-wishers: "Like prows and bows and bells they came, / clanging their metalled hides against a grief / that had dropped out from the pockets of the sky..." and their equally abrupt departure, evoked in this sure-footed pentameter: "And left their flowers to die before her eyes / as though they had not thought of her at all".

Richard Aaronowitz is fascinated by beginnings and endings. He adopts a conversational note rather at odds with the similes he likes to use. I enjoyed his 'Free Divers off Sardinia' and felt a strong sense of personality coming through. The same can be said of A.B. Jackson's demanding and ambitious work: direct, sharp in manner, with an intellectual edge, a valedictory quality. He is one of the few to approach anything vaguely religious, to open his eyes to the night sky beyond the farthest city light; his monologue, 'The Temptation of Saint Anthony' has welcome, if tortured, echoes of certain mid-century poets whose influence has never been really fully absorbed by later writers: Vernon Watkins, Thomas Blackburn, Jack Clemo...

Tabish Khair is in many ways the most traditional of the group. His is rich, aromatic, erotic poetry, unafraid to adopt a loftier note that poets of the British Isles might shun. Dignity, restraint and capital letters. Yet it is certainly not old-fashioned, though it prompts my rather hackneyed words of praise – beautiful, sensitive, musical.

The most original voice in the book is that of Kona MacPhee. Her biographical details alone suggest something surprising (born London, brought up in Australia: music student, motorbike mechanic, Web Architect...) and the poetry has a genuine lyricism and mystery, together with a bold experimental diction. There are invigorating formal pressures that sharpen her intelligence and she always has an eye to those wider, grander themes I mentioned earlier, an ear to the sounds the words make:

> A raven's restless mechanism
> ticks on the signal box. Below,
> midday sinuates the sheets of air
> that work their quavering mesmerism,
> dazing the land to stillness...
>
>   ('Terminus')

Bizarro's Bounty

SEAN O'BRIEN DETECTS CULTURAL IMPERIALISM IN A NEW ANTHOLOGY

Anthology of Twentieth Century British and Irish Poetry

Ed. Keith Tuma

Oxford University Press, $42.50
ISBN 0 19 512894X

POETRY IS TOO important to be left to zealots. Louis Simpson's great poem 'To the Western World' ends "And grave by grave we civilize the ground." The significance of this would not be lost on native Americans, or the Vietnamese, but in the absence of war a much more effective arm of "civilization" is everywhere in play, namely cultural imperialism. It was once said that Americans found no cultural differences so complex that they couldn't be overcome by ignoring them, and in a minor-outpost-in-the-badlands way, Keith Tuma's clodhopping anthology is part of this enterprise. We are to be made safe for Modernism. Apparently we've been denying its existence.

Tuma wants us to know he comes in friendship, to explain to us how things really are. As he notes, most of his readership will actually be college students in the USA, who won't know any better, but the introduction reads as though aimed at some readers in Britain and Ireland who may take issue with his approach. For them he has this warning:

Some...will be eager to point out that I am an American, and that my insistence that twentieth century British and Irish poetry be recognised for its contributions to modernism reflects American values. Forms of this insidious representational logic, in which national identity is paramount and citizenship magically confers authentic expertise, have had a devastating effect on much of the poetry produced in this century...[There] is... a problem with the use of reified or shallow notions of tradition to exclude whole ranges of poetry. The distorted rhetorics that

can result from an appeal to something like national tradition or "Englishness" have far-reaching consequences on both the reading and writing of poetry...

"Insidious representational logic", eh? Whereas Tuma has presumably acquired some one-size-fits-all insight which carries him beyond the reach of these ills. There are parallels here with George W. Bush's recent European visit. Admittedly Dubya had a missile shield to impose on his "freedom-loving allies", or else; Tuma only has poetry, but you can't fault his commitment to sharing the task of endarkenment. The inclination to the Left which might be inferred from this anthology – and which in a rational world would separate him from the Republican president (doh!) – serves merely to illustrate what happens in a country where the Left has no public political presence at all: it retires to college and tries to take over a shrivelled version of the world from there.

Tuma's enlightenment sounds as "reified and shallow" as what he condemns. The opposition he imagines is largely imaginary. There is no dominant notion of "Englishness" in English poetry, for example: insofar as it concerns poets, the meanings of the term are under continual discussion and revision. It is far more of an issue for Tuma, who feels the need to go on throwing (or snatching) off the Saxon yoke until the crack of doom, as though assuming that to be unconvinced by Olson means being in thrall to Betjeman – but hey, it's kinda complicated over here... As to "American values", they are, it seems, an unexamined good. In reality the "Englishness" of Larkin is very different from that of, say, Charles Tomlinson, or of Geoffrey Hill, who is in turn a very different reader of Englishness from Tony Harrison, who seems a long way from Jo Shapcott. As to Modernism, it meets no significant resistance, though Eliot and Stevens are probably more widely admired than Pound (and anyway Modernism is as much a European as an American phenomenon, something Tuma doesn't seem to acknowledge). Tuma adduces earlier anthologists,

Alvarez and Edward Lucie-Smith, to indicate English resistance to Modernism but the fact is that the post-1939 generations of poets have been receptive to many kinds of writing including Modernism, Postmodernism and the New York School, not to mention various branches of European poetry sufficiently engaged with history to have more on their minds than the ampersand and the reverse slash. The unsophisticated reader, though, might mistake the enduring concern for competence for an adherence to an insular "English" tradition. The poets, meanwhile, have seen Modernism as an enrichment of imaginative possibility, not as a new orthodoxy or a monument in need of polishing.

So: Modernism? No problem. On the other hand, there is a dislike of bad poems of any persuasion, as Tuma could have discovered if he'd bothered to ask anyone. (Anyone that is, apart from dear old Eric Jealous and E. K. Resentment, who normally can't get into the phone book, never mind an anthology). This anthology contains a good deal of work everyone should read, of course, but it's bloated by a large number of bad contemporary poems – including dull, pretentious, tin-eared, parasitic, fraudulent poems, poems whose only claim to verbal life is the vast support machine of allusion-by-numbers which turns them into inflated footnotes to their own sources. (The notes, heroically assembled by the editor's assistant, Nate Dorward, are many times more interesting than these poems). For every Roy Fisher there are ten Norbert Nomarks. If these people want to call themselves Modernist in their orientation, or Postmodernist, or "innovative", that's up to them and their sponsors, but here's a term which really embraces them: Post-imaginative. With the aid of a trainspotter's eye for the dictionary or the history book you could write a good deal of this stuff without the least glimmering of verbal ability or imaginative life – which suits its authors down to the ground. They have managed to find a rationale for elevating tedium into a virtue. The results will soon seem as dull and disposable as the talentless contemporaries of John Coltrane do in comparison with the real thing. What marks some of it out is that it's imitative of theory rather than practice. More interesting, and depressing, is the sense that for all the alleged avant-garde's opposition to capitalism, the work its poets produce is so often the dead simulacrum with which capitalism necessarily replaces the imagination – "important" but empty, "dissident" but monopolistic.

There are at any rate partial exceptions. Tom Raworth and Lee Harwood have their moments, as does the late John Riley, despite a glaring debt to Eliot. The late Barry MacSweeney has something rather more. Among the younger contributors, Helen McDonald (b. 1970) has an ear and an eye. You hope she'll shed the anachronism on which so much super-modernity relies. Caroline Bergvall (b.1964) has a smart way with a pun, though the trail of suggestion leads (in a way reminiscent of Roethke) back to the nursery: "a dirty doldo's / one fatpig / fruitcake / in the bowl of my pill". Now wash your hands.

Tuma also makes efforts to re-introduce older writers, but, for example, John Rodker, Nancy Cunard, Charles Madge, Clere Parsons and Nicholas Moore are largely of interest as historical curiosities, no more compelling in themselves than their Georgian or Movement equivalents. More peculiar is Tuma's decision to set his anthology's construction against that of Larkin's *Oxford Book*, as if anyone would seriously take Larkin's view as normative or canonical.

While accommodating a good deal of cack, the anthology offers Irish poetry without Michael Longley, Ciaran Carson, Tom Paulin and Nuala ni Dhomnaill, as well as wholly inadequate representation of MacNeice and Mahon; Scots poetry without Douglas Dunn, John Burnside, Don Paterson and Kathleen Jamie; and English poetry minus Ken Smith, Peter Porter (now fifty years a resident) and James Fenton. The omissions may not be wholly of the editor's choosing, but their seriouness should have warned Tuma against trying to pass this confection off as "a map". A map of what? Nowhere? Superman, the great American hero, used to be afflicted by a parallel being called Bizarro, who would escape now and again and – with the best of intentions – make a complete bollix of the universe. The Bizarros obviously need and deserve employment, but whether Oxford University Press should provide it is another matter.

Tuma alludes to a companion anthology, *Modern American Poetry*, edited by Cary Nelson. The contents of the other half of this pincer movement are instructive. For example, Ron Silliman gets more space than Wallace Stevens and Elizabeth Bishop. The American poet and critic William Logan, writing in *Parnassus,* had great sport with this, pointing out that those who make such choices lack the fear of God. They also lack a sense of humour, and it's the deep blankness in that area which makes Tuma's anthology such a laugh.

Residents Only?

by Martin Colthorpe

PETER SANSOM

Point of Sale

Carcanet, £6.95
ISBN 1 85754 484 6

JACKIE WILLS

Party

Leviathan, £8.00
ISBN 1 903563 04 6

IT IS OVER a year ago now since the Poetry Places scheme came to an end, but the poems are still coming to light in recently published collections. Peter Sansom's residency at Marks & Spencer was something of a classic – the humble poetry work-shopper caught in the glare of TV camera and corporate press conference – and the poems documenting the experience form the centrepiece of his third collection, *Point of Sale*. The opposition this sets up proves irresistible material for Sansom and his "verse diary" veers between his fascination – and discomfort – in an alien culture: "a finger buffet with me / all thumbs and foot in mouth" ('Manchester Airport for Belfast') and the familiar drudgery captured in 'Midland Mainline' which finds him "labouring back against the inertia / of coming into Bedford". The poems journey between actual places and through the course of surreal days but what underpins them is a restless soul searching. 'The Big Breakfast', a keynote amongst the residency poems, lurches from the The Holiday Inn "which looks like luxury you were meant for" to the TV studio where "I remember the Corrs / and being miked up, and talking, / making up verse, veering / between loving it / and can't-be-arsed, like most things / I do most days…" Particular poems focus on the writing workshops – a jaded subject perhaps – but one which suits Sansom's ability to find magic in the unlikeliest places. Occasionally they strike an obvious chord: "the commonplace miracle of people / saying who they are to people listening" ('Manchester Airport for Belfast') but sometimes the effect is breathtaking "for two hours / we go under for the polished stones / that once

home will have dried dull" ('The Poetry Society: Mont Blanc Workshop').

The residency poems provide an interesting contrast with the rest of the collection. Again place is important, but as a familiar – often nostalgic – backdrop, rather than as a new world for exploration. Sansom writes most effectively about the places which are dear to him, the provincial towns of his upbringing or rural places gilded with poetic history. The best examples are tender portraits of family life and love, with a strikingly intimate tone:

For a while you're this girl, sixteen,
just finished in the small hours
walking a mile across a frosty town
to a flat with french windows and a goldfish.

OK. But that ring,
thing what it cost before you lose it,
then lose it if you like, it's yours.

('Wye')

Tradition is important to Sansom and his poems ache with a sense of personal history that is constantly being retrieved from the flux of social change. His poems linger in a pre-Starbucks world of formica and Tizer, which, if overly sentimental, are reined in by self-awareness – in 'Chippie' he decides "Well yes, nostalgia's / not what it was". The poems are tinged with a sense of tragedy that affects our everyday lives – lost loved ones, a brother suffering from mental illness – and his writing gains its vitality from the tension between the desire to remember and the necessity of moving on.

In this collection, poems which tackle issues of weighty significance sit comfortably alongside those of quiet domesticity, and are linked by a remarkable evenness of tone. His style has a quiet authority characterised by well chosen line-breaks and rhyme which is used sparingly but appropriately. Above all, his ability to forge surprising images out of everyday domestic material stayed in my mind and made me warm to him:

your face still comes up
like a mismatch in the ring and you sneeze
without pause, your eyes heartbreak
or a broken tap.

('Hayfever')

This is Sansom's third collection from Carcanet, and his first for six years, in a published career spanning the last decade. Sansom is well known as a workshop leader and editor; *Point of Sale* is a timely reminder of his subtle poetic technique.

Jackie Wills is another poet with residencies recently added to her CV, having taken on the role at both the Countryside Agency and Lever Brothers under the Poetry Places scheme. The poems drawn from these experiences have a minimal presence in *Party* and amount to only the short poem 'Drought' (Lever Brothers) and the poem sequence 'North Downs Way' (Countryside Agency). The latter features a series of journeys which trace different paths across the North Downs, each poem closing with an incantatory recounting of places along the way. This literal mapping of people to a particular place, has more than a whiff of the commissioned poem about it, and feels restrained when compared to her best work.

Her poems artfully blur distinctions between present and past, between real and imagined characters and make quick metaphoric progressions which catch the reader by surprise. Sometimes these are well controlled, her husband coming to bed at three a.m enters "this breathy darkness the way / a peacock stalks around us at the end of a picnic" ('Peacock') before the poem shifts into lucid memory, with the peacock emblematic of another place and time. Moniza Alvi was right in saying that her poems "travel a long distance in a short space", but sometimes they left me straining to follow. 'Blue Mountains' is a good example of a poem which travels a long distance but also travels in too many directions, making it feel overcrowded, with its message obscured.

Wills is acutely aware of visual details which give her poems a vigourous quality as she moves from image to image. When her gaze rests for a moment it lends weight to the subject and the effects can be stunning. She writes very movingly about death. 'Windmills' focuses on the deaths of children and records in unflinching detail their burial ground:

> …..babies who stop
> moving in the womb; meningitis, cancer,
> cot deaths, the two girls murdered in Wild
> Park. Their stones are white marble
> back rests for waterlogged teddy bears

A series of poems about South Africa seem particularly suited to her technique, and have a great dramatic quality. Building up narrative through detailed observation, these poems edge their way

through a world charged with danger, whilst at the same time evoking a sense of a wider political significance.

> These are marshlands; even in high summer,
> jumping clumps of reedy grass you slip
> into unexpected springs. We're here to find
> your brother's grave
>
> ('Golden Highway')

In the title poem, a lifetime's worth of family and friends gather in a dreamlike fantasy, in an apt metaphor for the collection as a whole. This is a vast inventory of people and places recorded with clarity and precision. I found re-reading the poems a rewarding experience, bringing them into focus and revealing their power. This is a confident follow-up to 1995's *The Powder Tower*, which was shortlisted for the T S Eliot prize, and her work is deserving of wider recognition.